Communionis Notio

Preface
Alberto Bovone

Introduction
His Eminence Cardinal Joseph Ratzinger

Letter to the Bishops of the Catholic Church on Some Aspects of the Church Understood as Communion

Commentaries and Studies
S. Nagy—A.M. Sicari—L. Bouyer—F. Ocáriz—M. Thurian

The Church as Communion
On the First Anniversary of the Publication of the Letter
Communionis Notio

Libreria Editrice Vatican
United States Conference of Catholic Bishops
Washington, DC

English translation copyright © 2013, Libreria Editrice Vaticana. All rights reserved.

Scripture excerpts used in this work are taken from the *New American Bible*, rev. ed. © 2010, 1991, 1986, 1970 Confraternity of Christian Doctrine, Inc., Washington, DC. All rights reserved. No part of this work may be reproduced or transmitted in any form or by any means, electronic or mechanical, including photocopying, recording, or by any information storage and retrieval system, without permission in writing from the copyright owner.

Excerpts from *The Documents of Vatican II*, Walter M. Abbott, SJ, General Editor, copyright © 1966 by America Press, Inc. Reprinted with permission. All rights reserved.

Cover image, Tomas Abad / age fotostock

ISBN 978-1-60137-300-7

First printing, August 2013

Contents

Preface.. v

Introduction.. 1

Letter to the Bishops of the Catholic Church on Some Aspects of the Church Understood as Communion 6

COMMENTARIES AND STUDIES

The Church as Communion
  S. Nagy... 20

Universal Church and Particular Churches
  A.M. Sicari... 27

Communion of the Churches, Eucharist and Episcopacy
  L. Bouyer... 32

Unity and Diversity in Ecclesial Communion
  F. Ocáriz... 35

Ecclesial Communion and Ecumenism
  M. Thurian.. 38

The Church as Communion: On the First Anniversary of the Publication of the Letter Communionis Notio 43

Preface

This volume presents the *Letter to the Bishops of the Catholic Church on Some Aspects of the Church Understood as Communion*, promulgated by the Congregation for the Doctrine of the Faith on May 28, 1992, at the direction and with the approbation of Pope John Paul II.

The document was published in *Acta Apostolicae Sedis* (85 [1993], 838-850). It seeks to clarify the concept of "communion" on the basis of a correct ecclesiological reflection that promotes the deepening and understanding of faith and supports the efforts of theologians charged with the detailed examination of this aspect of the mystery of the Church. The word "communion" has become familiar, especially in the period following the Second Vatican Council, thanks to the broad popularity it has acquired not only in the writings of theologians but likewise in works of a popular nature, in periodicals of a Christian persuasion, and even in the language of preaching and liturgy. Still, it is well known that familiarity with a term does not mean grasping its meaning in the deepest sense, taken in all its essential dimensions. Thus the need has emerged for an authoritative exposition to establish the exact relationship between the word and the concept of communion in the Church. Such is the document's primary goal.

The text is preceded by an *Introduction* signed by Cardinal Joseph Ratzinger, prefect of the Congregation for the Doctrine of the Faith, which lays out the letter's meaning, importance, and basic outline.

There follow commentaries, originally published as articles in *L'Osservatore Romano*, which seek to illustrate the fundamental aspects treated by the document: Fr. Stanislao Nagy, *The Church as Communion*; Fr. Antonio Maria Sicari, *Universal Church and Particular Churches*; Fr. Louis Bouyer, *Communion of the Churches, Eucharist and Episcopacy*; Bishop Fernando Ocáriz, *Unity and Diversity in Ecclesial Communion*; and the Rev. Max Thurian, *Ecclesial Communion and Ecumenism*.

Reprinted by way of conclusion is the article *The Church as Communion: On the First Anniversary of the Publication of the Letter Communionis Notio*, originally published in *L'Osservatore Romano* on June 23, 1993, an assessment of the document's reception with a particular focus on the reactions raised to its more prominent points in Catholic and non-Catholic theological circles as well as in international ecumenical organizations. This article, countersigned with three asterisks, has an authoritative character.

✠ Alberto Bovone
Secretary

Introduction

1. The Significance and Importance of the Document

In the aftermath of the Second Vatican Council, the concept of "communion," referring to the Church, was one of the notions that most attracted the attention of theologians, along with the concept of the "People of God." Despite the noteworthy merits and the real steps forward in ecclesiological reflection during the post-Conciliar period, tendencies toward a reductive interpretation of these key concepts became apparent, entailing the danger of radically altering Catholic ecclesiology.

The expression "People of God" came more and more to be understood in the sense of a popular sovereignty; meanwhile the defining element of this people seemed to be simply forgotten, namely "God," the true sovereign of his "people" present in all the peoples of the world. Likewise apparent was a tendency to reduce the concept of "communion" to a more or less exclusively horizontal, sociological view. Such a view employs this word for an anti-hierarchical idea of a church that would actually be a federation of local churches taking precedence over the universal Church in every way.

The *goal* of the present document is to highlight the correct concept of "communion" following from the Second Vatican Council and the Extraordinary Synod of Bishops of 1985, where the bishops underscored anew how this category is pivotal for an adequate vision of the Church of God that is faithful to biblical teachings and to the patristic tradition (cf. no. 3). Thus the immediate *sources* of the document are the Council and the Synod of 1985, but the magisterial documents are used according to their individual intent for a deeper reading of the Bible and the Fathers and thus also for an adequate interpretation of the current ecclesiological reality.

The present document therefore presupposes that there are not isolated and juxtaposed ecclesiologies but that ultimately there exists only one *basic ecclesiology*, which can certainly be laid out and developed in different ways depending on how particular aspects are accentuated or highlighted. Such a diversity of systematic elaboration is legitimate and proper to the task of theology. Nevertheless, every sort of articulation must always be cognizant of the balance among the various essential elements of any ecclesiology that intends to be Catholic. In other words, if it is true that one can choose different points of departure and articulate systematic reflection on different concepts, it is likewise true that one must remain within the equilibrium of the authentic doctrinal tradition, preserving the integrity of the revealed data.

To avoid incomplete and inadequate interpretations therefore, the *Letter* of the Congregation for the Doctrine of the Faith seeks to safeguard the *criteria* for a correct understanding of the notion of "communion" by explaining it precisely under three fundamental aspects:

a) The concept of "communion" as it relates to other central ecclesiological notions such as "People of God," "body of Christ," and "sacrament"
b) The concept of "communion" as it relates to the Eucharist and to the episcopacy, thus pinpointing the meaning of the unity of the Church expressed in the reciprocal interiority between the universal Church and particular Churches
c) The concept of "communion" as it relates to the bond among the bishops and between them and the Successor of Peter, which is the visible foundation of the unity of the Church, mindful of the caution and concerns raised by an ecumenical perspective.

2. The Essential Outline of the Document

The document's five chapters focus on five points.

1. First of all, it recognizes that the notion of communion quite adequately expresses the profound nucleus of the mystery of the Church. This notion entails both the *vertical dimension* (communion with God) and the *horizontal* (communion among men), both the *invisible dimension* (intimate communion with the Most Holy Trinity and with the other people) and the *visible* (communion in the doctrine of the Apostles, in the sacraments, and in the hierarchical order). Therefore, this communion is not merely moral or psychological in nature but rather ontological and supernatural, and it implies a spiritual solidarity among the members of the Church inasmuch as they are members of a single body; namely, the Body of Christ.

It is important to note in this context how forcefully the document accentuates the self-transcendence of the Church, which is not an entity turned in on itself but rather open to missionary and ecumenical endeavor, since she is sent into the world to announce and to bear witness (no. 4).

2. Secondly, it considers the concrete expressions of the mystery of the Church understood as communion.

The concept of communion is applied, first of all, to the reality of the particular Churches which are, however, real "Churches" inasmuch as they are constituted in the image of the universal Church. Consequently, every particular Church is really Church inasmuch as the one, holy, catholic, and apostolic Church is present and active in it. This means that *the Church of Christ cannot be understood as a sum or a federation of particular Churches*. In its essential mystery, the universal Church is "ontologically and temporally prior to every individual particular Church" (no. 9), and these take their origin from her.

Following Scripture and the Fathers, the document highlights this double priority of the universal Church. The divine idea of his Church to be created in history is singular: his Bride, his City, the heavenly Jerusalem, his one people from Abraham until the last of the chosen. Following Jewish traditions, the Fathers speak about the preexistence of this City of God before the creation of the world, and the interior goal of creation is, in fact, this definitive city, the place where God's will is realized and earth becomes heaven.

This ideal precedence of the one universal Church is also expressed as a temporal precedence on the day of Pentecost: the apostolic community gathered around Mary and transformed by the Holy Spirit into a Church is not the local Church of Jerusalem. Every Apostle has a universal mission, and all of them together are the one nascent Church. Therefore, the particular Churches are born out of their preaching, beginning with the Church of Jerusalem. They are all daughters and concretizations of the universal Church which, by speaking all languages, shows itself to be *catholic* already in the first moment of its existence; that is, the one People of God gathered out of all the peoples of the world.

In this context, the document underscores the universal "catholic" character of baptism. In its sacramental substance, baptism is not admission into some local community but rather incorporation into the one body of Christ. Anyone who is baptized belongs to the Church wherever he or she goes, or, as the document so beautifully puts it, "In the Church no one is a stranger" (no. 10). In all places and in all languages she is always the same Church, the one Bride of Christ.

3. Thirdly, the concept of communion is related to the unity of the Church on one hand and to the Eucharist and the episcopacy on the other. Communion among the Churches in the unity of the universal Church is *rooted in the Eucharist*, because the celebration of the Eucharistic sacrifice in a particular or local community is never a celebration of that community alone. It becomes Church uniquely through receiving the entire sacramental gift of grace and through communion with the one, indivisible Eucharistic

Body of the Lord, which implies the unity and indivisibility of his mystical Body, which is the Church.

Thus, the unity of the Church is also *rooted in the episcopacy*. In fact, just as the very idea of a *body of Churches* recalls the existence of a Church that is Head of the Churches, namely the Church of Rome, so too the unity of the episcopacy entails the existence of a Head Bishop of the *Body or College of Bishops*, namely the Roman Pontiff.

The unity of the Eucharist and the unity of the episcopacy are not extrinsic realities or organizational principles with regard to the unity of the Church; they are rather theological realities, reciprocally linked and intrinsic to the mystery of the Church itself.

4. Furthermore, this unity of the Church does not stand in the way of plurality and diversity in respect to the diversity of ministries, of charisms, and of the various forms of apostolate. It is not just that the promotion of unity and of plurality are not opposed to each other; rather they mutually enrich each other to the degree that they look forward together to building up the one body of Christ that is the Church by means of charity, which is the bond of perfection. In this context, we can understand and justify those institutions and communities that are established by the apostolic authority and as such belong to the universal Church, even though its members also remain members of the particular Churches; likewise the many religious institutes and societies of apostolic life that belong to the life and sanctity of the Church even though they do not form part of its hierarchical structure.

5. Finally, the ecclesiological concept of communion has weighty *ecumenical implications*.

From the logic of the document it follows that the succession in the ministry of Peter, the visible expression of responsibility for the unity of communion, the unity of the Eucharistic Body from which the one body of the Church is born as the body of Christ, is not a purely organizational reality external to the true essence of communion itself—being the Church of the Lord. At the same time, the document underscores the ecumenical concept of the Council's ecclesiology and speaks of the many elements of the Church of Christ that are present in other, non-Catholic churches and ecclesial communities—elements that "allow us, amid joy and hope, to acknowledge the existence of a certain communion, albeit imperfect" (no. 17).

By underlining this doctrinal principle, the letter intends to clarify further the nature of this "imperfect communion," to which end it distinguishes the relationship of communion with the Orthodox Churches and with the reformed communities.

The Orthodox Churches, although separated from communion with the Successor of Peter, remain united with the Catholic Church by means of the closest bonds, such as the apostolic succession and a valid Eucharist, and therefore merit the title of particular Churches, as Vatican II already taught. Nevertheless, the principle remains valid that the unity of the Church expressed in the Petrine ministry is not an external adjunct to particular Churches already complete in themselves and self-sufficient. Such unity is rather a defining principle of the particular Church as such. Consequently, the document says that "the situation of those venerable Christian communities also means that their existence as particular Churches is wounded" (no. 17).

This wound is even deeper in those ecclesial communities that have not preserved the apostolic succession on which the validity of the Eucharist depends.

To understand the passionate ecumenical commitment of the present document, it is important to note that the text frankly recognizes *that such a situation also implies a wound for the Catholic Church*, albeit different in nature, inasmuch as it stands in the way of fully realizing her universality in history. Hence it is necessary to press on energetically in ecumenical endeavors at the heart of which heart, according to our text, is a renewed conversion to the Lord. The document expresses the hope that, in the light and strength of such a conversion, it might be possible for everyone to recognize the primacy of Peter in his successors, the Bishops of Rome, and to see the Petrine ministry carried out as the Lord intended, as universal apostolic service, present within all the particular Churches, and which, while preserving its substance and identity as a divine institution, can also express itself in different forms, depending on circumstances of time and place, as historical development shows.

With the present *Letter*, the Congregation for the Doctrine of the Faith has sought to offer the bishops, theologians, and all the faithful of the People of God an authoritative doctrinal contribution so that the communion of believers in all times and places might be lived not merely as a horizontal and external element but as an interior grace and, at the same time, as a visible sign of the gift of the Lord, which can only make unity a reality by overcoming every boundary and every limitation due to sin and human weakness.

Cardinal Joseph Ratzinger

Letter to the Bishops of the Catholic Church on Some Aspects of the Church Understood as Communion

Introduction

1. The concept of *communion* (*koinonía*), which appears with a certain prominence in the texts of the Second Vatican Council,[1] is very suitable for expressing the core of the Mystery of the Church, and can certainly be a key for the renewal of Catholic ecclesiology.[2] A deeper appreciation of the fact that the Church is a Communion is, indeed, a task of special importance, which provides ample latitude for theological reflection on the mystery of the Church, "*whose nature is such that it always admits new and deeper exploring.*"[3] However, some approaches to ecclesiology suffer from a clearly inadequate awareness of the Church as a *mystery of communion*, especially insofar as they have not sufficiently integrated the concept of *communion* with the concepts of *People of God* and of the *Body of Christ*, and have not given due importance to the relationship between the Church as *communion* and the Church as *sacrament*.

2. Bearing in mind the doctrinal, pastoral and ecumenical importance of the different aspects regarding the Church understood as Communion, the Congregation for the Doctrine of the Faith has considered it opportune, by means of this *Letter*, to recall briefly and to clarify, where necessary, some of the fundamental elements that are to be considered already settled also by those who undertake the hoped-for theological investigation.

---

1 Cf. Constitution *Lumen Gentium*, nos. 4, 8, 13-15, 18, 21, 24-25; Constitution *Dei Verbum*, no. 10; Constitution *Gaudium et Spes*, no. 32; Decree *Unitatis Redintegratio*, nos. 2-4, 14-15, 17-19, 22.
2 Cf. Synod of Bishops, Second Extraordinary Assembly (1985), *Relatio Finalis*, II, C), 1.
3 Paul VI, *Opening Address for the Second Period of the Second Vatican Council*, 29-IX-1963: AAS 55 (1963) p. 848. Cf., for example, the perspectives for further reflection indicated by the International Theological Commission, in its *Themata Selecta de Ecclesiologia*: "Documenta (1969-1985)," Libreria Editrice Vaticana 1988, pp. 462-559.

I. The Church, a Mystery of Communion

3. The concept of *communion* lies *"at the heart of the Church's self-understanding,"*[4] insofar as it is the Mystery of the personal union of each human being with the divine Trinity and with the rest of mankind, initiated with the faith,[5] and, having begun as a reality in the Church on earth, is directed toward its eschatological fulfillment in the heavenly Church.[6]

If the concept of *communion*, which is not a univocal concept, is to serve as a key to ecclesiology, it has to be understood within the teaching of the Bible and the patristic tradition, in which *communion* always involves a double dimension: the *vertical* (communion with God) and the *horizontal* (communion among men). It is essential to the Christian understanding of *communion* that it be recognized above all as a gift from God, as a fruit of God's initiative carried out in the Paschal Mystery. The new relationship between man and God, that has been established in Christ and is communicated through the sacraments, also extends to a new relationship among human beings. As a result, the concept of *communion* should be such as to express both the sacramental nature of the Church while *"we are away from the Lord,"*[7] and also the particular unity which makes the faithful into members of one and the same Body, the Mystical Body of Christ,[8] an organically structured community,[9] *"a people brought into one by the unity of the Father and of the Son and of the Holy Spirit,"*[10] and endowed with suitable means for its visible and social union.[11]

4. *Ecclesial communion is at the same time both invisible and visible.* As an invisible reality, it is the communion of each human being with the Father through Christ in the Holy Spirit, and with the others who are fellow sharers

---

4   John Paul II, *Address to the Bishops of the United States of America*, 16-IX-1987, no. 1: "Insegnamenti di Giovanni Paolo II" X, 3 (1987) p. 553.
5   1 Jn 1:3: *"That which we have seen and heard, we proclaim also to you, so that you may have fellowship with us; and our fellowship is with the Father and with his Son Jesus Christ."* Cf. also 1 Cor 1:9; John Paul II, Apostolic Exhortation *Christifideles Laici*, 30-XII-1988, no. 19, Synod of Bishops (1985), *Relatio Finalis*, II, C), 1.
6   Cf. Phil 3:20-21; Col 3:1-4; Constitution *Lumen Gentium*, no. 48.
7   2 Cor 5:6. Cf. Constitution *Lumen Gentium*, no. 1.
8   Cf. *ibidem*, no. 7; Pius XII, Encyclical *Mystici Corporis*, 29-VI-1943: AAS 35 (1943) pp. 200ff.
9   Cf. Constitution *Lumen Gentium*, no. 11/a.
10 St. Cyprian, *De Oratione Dominica*, 23: PL 4, 553; cf. Constitution *Lumen Gentium*, no. 4/b.
11 Cf. Constitution *Lumen Gentium*, no. 9/c.

in the divine nature,[12] in the passion of Christ,[13] in the same faith,[14] in the same spirit.[15] In the Church on earth, there is an intimate relationship between this invisible communion and the visible communion in the teaching of the Apostles, in the sacraments and in the hierarchical order. By means of these divine gifts, which are very visible realities, Christ carries out in different ways in history his prophetical, priestly and kingly *function* for the salvation of mankind.[16] This link between the invisible and visible elements of ecclesial communion constitutes the Church as the *Sacrament* of salvation.

From this sacramentality it follows that the Church is not a reality closed in on herself; rather, she is permanently open to missionary and ecumenical endeavor, for she is sent to the world to announce and witness, to make present and spread the mystery of communion which is essential to her: to gather together all people and all things into Christ;[17] so as to be for all an *"inseparable sacrament of unity."*[18]

5. Ecclesial communion, into which each individual is introduced by faith and by Baptism,[19] has its root and center in the Blessed Eucharist. Indeed, Baptism is an incorporation into a body that the risen Lord builds up and keeps alive through the Eucharist, so that this body can truly be called the Body of Christ. The Eucharist is the creative force and source of *communion* among the members of the Church, precisely because it unites each one of them with Christ himself: *"Really sharing in the body of the Lord in the breaking of the eucharistic bread, we are taken up into communion with him and with one another. 'Because the bread is one, we, though many, are one body, all of us who partake of the one bread' (1 Cor 10:17)."*[20]

Hence, the Pauline expression *the Church is the Body of Christ* means that the Eucharist, in which the Lord gives us his Body and transforms us into one

---

12 Cf. 2 Pt 1:4.
13 Cf. 2 Cor 1:7.
14 Cf. Eph 4:13; Philem 6.
15 Cf. Phil 2:1.
16 Cf. Constitution *Lumen Gentium*, nos. 25-27.
17 Cf. Mt 28:19-20; Jn 17:21-23; Eph 1:10; Constitution *Lumen Gentium*, nos. 9/b, 13 and 17; Decree *Ad Gentes*, nos. 1 and 5; St. Irenaeus, *Adversus Haereses*, III, 16, 6 and 22, 1-3: PG 7, 925-926 and 955-958.
18 St. Cyprian, *Epist. ad Magnum*, 6: PL 3, 1142.
19 Eph 4, 4-5: "*There is one body and one Spirit, just as you were called to the one hope that belongs to your call, one Lord, one faith, one baptism.*" Cf. also Mk 16:16.
20 Constitution *Lumen Gentium*, no. 7/b. The Eucharist is the sacrament "*through which in the present age the Church is made*" (St. Augustine, *Contra Faustum*, 12, 20: PL 42, 265). "*Our sharing in the body and blood of Christ leads to no other end than that of transforming us into that which we receive*" (St. Leo the Great, *Sermo* 63, 7: PL 54, 357).

Body,[21] is where the Church expresses herself permanently in most essential form. While present everywhere, she is yet only *one*, just as Christ is *one*.

6. The Church is a *Communion of the saints*, to use a traditional expression that is found in the Latin versions of the Apostles' Creed from the end of the fourth century.[22] The common visible sharing in the goods of salvation (*the holy things*), and especially in the Eucharist, is the source of the invisible communion among the sharers (*the saints*). This communion brings with it a spiritual solidarity among the members of the Church, insofar as they are members of one same Body,[23] and it fosters their effective union in charity by constituting "*one heart and soul.*"[24] Communion tends also toward union in prayer,[25] inspired in all by one and the same Spirit,[26] the Holy Spirit "*who fills and unites the whole Church.*"[27]

In its invisible elements, this communion exists not only among the members of the pilgrim Church on earth, but also between these and all who, having passed from this world in the grace of the Lord, belong to the heavenly Church or will be incorporated into it after having been fully purified.[28] This means, among other things, that there is a *mutual relationship* between the pilgrim Church on earth and the heavenly Church in the historical-redemptive mission. Hence the ecclesiological importance not only of Christ's intercession on behalf of his members,[29] but also of that of the saints and, in an eminent fashion, of the Blessed Virgin Mary's.[30] *Devotion to the saints*, which is such a strong feature of the piety of the Christian people, can thus be seen to correspond in its very essence to the profound reality of the Church as a mystery of communion.

---

21 Cf. Constitution *Lumen Gentium*, nos. 3 and 11/a; St. John Chrysostom, *In 1 Cor. hom.*, 24, 2: PG 61, 200.
22 Cf. Denz.-Schön. 19, 26-30.
23 Cf. 1 Cor 12:25-27; Eph 1:22-23; 3:3-6.
24 Acts 4:32.
25 Cf. Acts 2:42.
26 Cf. Rom 8:15-16.26; Gal 4:6; Constitution *Lumen Gentium*, no. 4.
27 St. Thomas Aquinas, *De Veritate*, q. 29, a. 4 c. Indeed, "*lifted up on the cross and glorified, the Lord Jesus poured forth the Spirit whom he had promised, and through whom he has called and gathered together the people of the New Covenant, which is the Church, into a unity of faith, hope and charity*" (Decree *Unitatis Redintegratio*, no. 2/b).
28 Cf. Constitution *Lumen Gentium*, no. 49.
29 Cf. Heb 7:25.
30 Cf. Constitution *Lumen Gentium*, nos. 50 and 66.

II. Universal Church and Particular Churches

7. The *Church of Christ*, which we profess in the Creed to be one, holy, catholic and apostolic, is the universal Church, that is, the worldwide community of the disciples of the Lord,[31] which is present and active amid the particular characteristics and the diversity of persons, groups, times and places. Among these manifold particular expressions of the saving presence of the one Church of Christ, there are to be found, from the times of the Apostles on, those entities which are in themselves *Churches*,[32] because, although they are particular, the universal Church becomes present in them with all its essential elements.[33] They are therefore constituted "*after the model of the universal Church*,"[34] and each of them is "*a portion of the People of God entrusted to a bishop to be guided by him with the assistance of his clergy.*"[35]

8. The universal Church is therefore the *Body of the Churches*.[36] Hence it is possible to apply the concept of communion *in analogous fashion* to the union existing among particular Churches, and to see the universal Church as a *Communion of Churches*. Sometimes, however, the idea of a "communion of particular Churches" is presented in such a way as to weaken the concept of the unity of the Church at the visible and institutional level. Thus it is asserted that every particular Church is a subject complete in itself, and that the universal Church is the result of a *reciprocal recognition* on the part of the particular Churches. This ecclesiological unilateralism, which impoverishes not only the concept of the universal Church but also that of the particular Church, betrays an insufficient understanding of the concept of communion. As history shows, when a particular Church has sought to become self-sufficient, and has weakened its real communion with the universal Church and with its living and visible center, its internal unity suffers too, and it finds itself in danger of losing its own freedom in the face of the various forces of slavery and exploitation.[37]

9. In order to grasp the true meaning of the analogical application of the term *communion* to the particular Churches taken as a whole, one must bear

---

31 Cf. Mt 16:18; 1 Cor 12:28; etc.
32 Cf. Acts 8:1; 11:22; 1 Cor 1:2; 16:19; Gal 1:22; Rev 2:1.8; etc.
33 Cf. Pontifical Biblical Commission, *Unité et diversité dans l'Eglise*, Libreria Editrice Vaticana 1989, especially, pp. 14-28.
34 Constitution *Lumen Gentium*, no. 23/a; cf. Decree *Ad Gentes*, no. 20/a.
35 Decree *Christus Dominus*, no. 11/a.
36 Constitution *Lumen Gentium*, no. 23/b. Cf. St. Hilary Of Poitiers, *In Psalm.*, 14, 3: PL 9, 301; St. Gregory the Great, *Moralia*, IV, 7, 12: PL 75, 643.
37 Cf. Paul VI, Apostolic Exhortation *Evangelii Nuntiandi*, 8-XII-1975, no. 64/b.

in mind above all that the particular Churches, insofar as they are *"part of the one Church of Christ,"*[38] have a special relationship of *"mutual interiority"*[39] with the whole, that is, with the universal Church, because in every particular Church *"the one, holy, catholic and apostolic Church of Christ is truly present and active."*[40] For this reason, *"the universal Church cannot be conceived as the sum of the particular Churches, or as a federation of particular Churches."*[41] It is not the result of the communion of the Churches, but, in its essential mystery, it is a reality *ontologically and temporally* prior to every *individual* particular Church.

Indeed, according to the Fathers, *ontologically*, the Church-mystery, the Church that is one and unique, precedes creation,[42] and gives birth to the particular Churches as her daughters. She expresses herself in them; she is the mother and not the product of the particular Churches. Furthermore, the Church is manifested, *temporally*, on the day of Pentecost in the community of the one hundred and twenty gathered around Mary and the twelve Apostles, the representatives of the one unique Church and the founders-to-be of the local Churches, who have a mission directed to the world: from the first the Church *speaks all languages*.[43]

From the Church, which in its origins and its first manifestation is universal, have arisen the different local Churches, as particular expressions of the one unique Church of Jesus Christ. Arising *within* and *out of* the universal Church, they have their ecclesiality in it and from it. Hence the formula of the Second Vatican Council: *The Church in and formed out of the Churches (Ecclesia in et ex Ecclesiis),*[44] is inseparable from this other formula: *The*

---

38   Decree *Christus Dominus*, no. 6/c.
39   John Paul II, *Address to the Roman Curia*, 20-XII-1990, no. 9: *L'Osservatore Romano*, 21-XII-1990, p. 5.
40   Decree *Christus Dominus*, no. 11/a.
41   John Paul II, *Address to the Bishops of the United States of America*, 16-IX-1987, no. 3: as quoted, p. 555.
42   Cf. Shepherd of Hermas, *Vis.* 2, 4: PG 2, 897-900; St. Clement of Rome, *Epist. II ad Cor.*, 14, 2: Funck, 1, 200.
43   Cf. Acts 2, 1ff. St. Irenacus, *Adversus Haereses*, III, 17, 2 (PG 7, 929-930): "At Pentecost (. . .) all nations (. . .) had become a marvelous choir to intone a hymn of praise to God in perfect harmony, because the Holy Spirit had brought distances to naught, eliminated discordant notes and transformed the varieties of the peoples into the first-fruits to be offered to the Father." Cf. also St. Fulgentius of Ruspe, *Sermo 8 in Pentecoste*, 2-3: PL 65, 743-744.
44   Constitution *Lumen Gentium*, no. 23/a: "*It is in these and formed out of them that the one and unique Catholic Church exists.*" This doctrine develops in the same line of continuity what had been stated previously, for example by Pius X, Encyclical *Mystici Corporis*, as quoted, p. 211: "Out of which the one Catholic Church exists and is composed."

Churches in and formed out of the Church (Ecclesia in et ex Ecclesiis).[45] Clearly the relationship between the universal Church and the particular Churches is a mystery, and cannot be compared to that which exists between the whole and the parts in a purely human group or society.

10. Every member of the faithful, through faith and Baptism, is inserted into the one, holy, catholic and apostolic Church. He or she does not belong to the universal Church in a *mediate* way, *through* belonging to a particular Church, but in an *immediate* way, even though entry into and life within the universal Church are necessarily brought about *in* a particular Church. From the point of view of the Church understood as communion, this means therefore that the universal *communion of the faithful* and the *communion of the Churches* are not consequences of one another, but constitute the same reality seen from different viewpoints.

Moreover, one's *belonging* to a particular Church never conflicts with the reality that *in the Church no one is a stranger*:[46] each member of the faithful, especially in the celebration of the Eucharist, is in *his or her* Church, in the Church of Christ, regardless of whether or not he or she belongs, according to canon law, to the diocese, parish or other particular community where the celebration takes place. In this sense, without impinging on the necessary regulations regarding juridical dependence,[47] whoever belongs to one particular Church belongs to all the Churches; since belonging to the *Communion*, like belonging to the Church, is never simply particular, but by its very nature is always universal.[48]

III. Communion of the Churches, Eucharist and Episcopate

11. Unity, or communion, between the particular Churches in the universal Church, is rooted not only in the same faith and in the common Baptism, but above all in the Eucharist and in the Episcopate.

It is rooted in the Eucharist because the eucharistic Sacrifice, while always performed in a particular community, is never a celebration of that community alone. In fact, the community, in receiving the eucharistic presence of the Lord, receives the entire gift of salvation and shows, even in its

---

45 Cf. John Paul II, *Address to the Roman Curia*, 20-XII-1990, no. 9: as quoted, p. 5.
46 Cf. Gal 3:28.
47 Cf., for example, CIC, c. 107.
48 St. John Chrysostom, *In Ioann. hom.*, 65, 1 (PG 59, 361): "*Whoever is in Rome knows that the Indians are his members.*" Cf. Constitution *Lumen Gentium*, no. 13/b.

lasting visible particular form, that it is the image and true presence of the one, holy, catholic and apostolic Church.[49]

The rediscovery of a *eucharistic ecclesiology*, though being of undoubted value, has however sometimes placed unilateral emphasis on the principle of the local Church. It is claimed that, where the Eucharist is celebrated, the totality of the mystery of the Church would be made present in such a way as to render any other principle of unity or universality non-essential. Other conceptions, under different theological influences, present this particular view of the Church in an even more radical form, going as far as to hold that gathering together in the name of Jesus (cf. Mt 18:20) is the same as generating the Church: the assembly which in the name of Christ becomes a community, would hold within itself the powers of the Church, including power as regards the Eucharist. The Church, some say, would arise "from base level." These and other similar errors do not take sufficiently into account that it is precisely the Eucharist that renders all self-sufficiency on the part of the particular Churches impossible. Indeed, the unicity and indivisibility of the eucharistic Body of the Lord implies the unicity of his mystical Body, which is the one and indivisible Church. From the eucharistic center arises the necessary openness of every celebrating community, of every particular Church; by allowing itself to be drawn into the open arms of the Lord, it achieves insertion into his one and undivided Body. For this reason too, the existence of the Petrine ministry, which is a foundation of the unity of the Episcopate and of the universal Church, bears a profound correspondence to the eucharistic character of the Church.

12. In fact, the unity of the Church is also rooted in the unity of the Episcopate.[50] As the very idea of the *Body of the Churches* calls for the existence of a Church that is *Head* of the Churches, which is precisely the Church of Rome, *"foremost in the universal communion of charity,"*[51] so too the unity of the Episcopate involves the existence of a Bishop who is Head of the *Body or College of Bishops*, namely the Roman Pontiff.[52] Of the unity of the Episcopate, as also of the unity of the entire Church, *"the Roman Pontiff, as the successor of Peter, is a perpetual and visible source and foundation."*[53] This unity of the

---

49 Cf. Constitution *Lumen Gentium*, no. 26/a; St. Augustine, *In Ioann. Ev. Tract.*, 26, 13: PL 35, 1612-1613.
50 Cf. Constitution *Lumen Gentium*, nos. 18/b, 21/b. 22/a. Cf. also St. Cyprian, *De Unitate Ecclesiae*, 5: PL 4, 516-517; St. Augustine, *In Ioann. Ev. Tract.*, 46, 5: PL 35, 1730.
51 St. Ignatius Of Antioch, *Epist. ad Rom.*, prol.: PG 5, 685; cf. Constitution *Lumen Gentium*, no. 13/c.
52 Cf. Constitution *Lumen Gentium*, no. 22/b.
53 *Ibidem*, no. 23/a. Cf. Constitution *Pastor Aeternus*: Denz.-Schön. 3051-3057; St. Cyprian,

Episcopate is perpetuated through the centuries by means of the *apostolic succession*, and is also the foundation of the identity of the Church of every age with the Church built by Christ upon Peter and upon the other Apostles.[54]

13. The Bishop is a visible source and foundation of the unity of the particular Church entrusted to his pastoral ministry.[55] But for each particular Church to be fully Church, that is, the particular presence of the universal Church with all its essential elements, and hence constituted *after the model of the universal Church*, there must be present in it, as a proper element, the supreme authority of the Church: the Episcopal College "*together with their head, the Supreme Pontiff, and never apart from him.*"[56] The Primacy of the Bishop of Rome and the episcopal College are proper elements of the universal Church that are "*not derived from the particularity of the Churches,*"[57] but are nevertheless *interior* to each particular Church. Consequently "*we must see the ministry of the Successor of Peter, not only as a 'global' service, reaching each particular Church from 'outside', as it were, but as belonging already to the essence of each particular Church from 'within.'*"[58] Indeed, the ministry of the Primacy involves, in essence, a truly episcopal power, which is not only supreme, full and universal, but also *immediate*, over everybody, whether Pastors or other faithful.[59] The ministry of the Successor of Peter as something *interior* to each particular Church is a necessary expression of that fundamental *mutual interiority* between universal Church and particular Church.[60]

14. The unity of the Eucharist and the unity of the Episcopate *with Peter and under Peter* are not independent roots of the unity of the Church, since Christ instituted the Eucharist and the Episcopate as essentially interlinked realities.[61] The Episcopate is *one*, just as the Eucharist is *one*: the one Sacrifice of the one Christ, dead and risen. The liturgy expresses this reality in various ways, showing, for example, that every celebration of the Eucharist is

---

De Unitate Ecclesiae, 4: PL 4, 512-515.
54   Cf. Constitution *Lumen Gentium*, no. 20; St. Irenaeus, *Adversus Haereses*, III, 3, 1-3: PG 7, 848-849; St. Cyprian, *Epist*. 27, 1: PL 4, 305-306; St. Augustine, *Contra advers. legis et prophet.*, 1, 20, 39: PL 42, 626.
55   Cf. Constitution *Lumen Gentium*, no. 23/a.
56   *Ibidem*, no. 22/b; cf also no. 19.
57   John Paul II, *Address to the Roman Curia*, 20-XII-1990, no. 9: as quoted, p. 5.
58   John Paul II, *Address to the Bishops of the United States of America*, 16-IX-1987, no. 4: as quoted, p. 556.
59   Cf. Constitution *Pastor Aeternus*, chap. 3: Denz.-Schön 3064; Constitution *Lumen Gentium*, no. 22/b.
60   Cf. *supra*, no. 9.
61   Cf. Constitution *Lumen Gentium*, no. 26; St. Ignatius of Antioch, *Epist. ad Philadel.*, 4: PG 5, 700; *Epist. ad Smyrn.*, 8: PG 5, 713.

performed in union not only with the proper Bishop, but also with the Pope, with the episcopal order, with all the clergy, and with the entire people.[62] Every valid celebration of the Eucharist expresses this universal communion *with Peter* and with the whole Church, or *objectively* calls for it, as in the case of the Christian Churches separated from Rome.[63]

IV. Unity and Diversity in Ecclesial Communion

15. *"The universality of the Church involves, on the one hand, a most solid unity, and on the other, a plurality and a diversification, which do not obstruct unity, but rather confer upon it the character of 'communion.'"*[64] This plurality refers both to the diversity of ministries, charisms, and forms of life and apostolate within each particular Church, and to the diversity of traditions in liturgy and culture among the various particular Churches.[65]

Fostering a unity that does not obstruct diversity, and acknowledging and fostering a diversification that does not obstruct unity but rather enriches it, is a fundamental task of the Roman Pontiff for the whole Church,[66] and without prejudice to the general law of the Church itself, of each Bishop in the particular Church entrusted to his pastoral ministry.[67] But the building up and safeguarding of this unity, on which diversification confers the character of communion, is also a task of everyone in the Church, because all are called to build it up and preserve it each day, above all by means of that charity which is *"the bond of perfection."*[68]

16. For a more complete vision of this aspect of ecclesial communion—unity in diversity—one needs to bear in mind that there are institutions and communities established by the Apostolic Authority for specific pastoral tasks. They belong *as such* to the universal Church, though their members are also members of the particular Churches where they live and work. The manner of belonging to the particular Churches, with its own particular

---

62 Cf. *Roman Missal*, Eucharistic Prayer III.
63 Cf. Constitution *Lumen Gentium*, no. 8/b.
64 John Paul II, *Address*, General Audience, 27-IX-1989, no. 2: "Insegnamenti di Giovanni Paolo II" XII, 2 (1989) p. 679.
65 Cf. Constitution *Lumen Gentium*, no. 23/d.
66 Cf. *ibidem*, no. 13/c.
67 Cf. Decree *Christus Dominus*, no. 8/a.
68 Col 3:14. St. Thomas Aquinas, *Exposit. in Symbol. Apost.*, a. 9: *"The Church is one (. . .) through the unity of charity, because all are joined in the love of God, and among themselves in mutual love."*

flexibility,⁶⁹ takes different juridical forms. But it does not erode the unity of the particular Church founded on the Bishop; rather, it helps endow this unity with the interior diversification which is a feature of *communion*.⁷⁰

In the context of the Church understood as communion, consideration should also be given to the many institutes and societies that express the charisms of consecrated life and apostolic life, with which the Holy Spirit enriches the Mystical Body of Christ. Although these do not belong to the hierarchical structure of the Church, they belong to its life and holiness.⁷¹

Given their supradiocesan character, rooted in the Petrine ministry, all these ecclesial realities are also elements at the service of communion among the various particular Churches.

V. Ecclesial Communion and Ecumenism

17. "*The Church knows that she is joined in many ways to the baptized who are honored by the name of Christian, but who do not however profess the Catholic faith in its entirety or have not preserved unity or communion under the successor of Peter.*"⁷² Among the non-Catholic Churches and Christian communities, there are indeed to be found many elements of the Church of Christ, which allow us, amid joy and hope, to acknowledge the existence of a certain communion, albeit imperfect.⁷³

This communion exists especially with the Eastern orthodox Churches, which, though separated from the See of Peter, remain united to the Catholic Church by means of very close bonds, such as the apostolic succession and a valid Eucharist, and therefore merit the title of particular Churches.⁷⁴ Indeed, "*through the celebration of the Eucharist of the Lord in each of these Churches, the Church of God is built up and grows in stature*,"⁷⁵ for in every valid celebration of the Eucharist the one, holy, catholic and apostolic Church becomes truly present.⁷⁶

Since, however, communion with the universal Church, represented by Peter's Successor, is not an external complement to the particular Church,

---

69   Cf. *supra*, no. 10.
70   Cf. *supra*, no. 15.
71   Cf. Constitution *Lumen Gentium*, no. 44/d.
72   Constitution *Lumen Gentium*, no. 15.
73   Cf. Decree *Unitatis Redintegratio*, nos. 3/a and 22; see also Constitution *Lumen Gentium*, no. 13/d.
74   Cf. Decree *Unitatis Redintegratio*, nos. 14 and 15/c.
75   *Ibidem*, no. 15/a.
76   Cf. *supra*, nos. 5 and 14.

but one of its internal constituents, the situation of those venerable Christian communities also means that their existence as particular Churches is *wounded*. The wound is even deeper in those ecclesial communities which have not retained the apostolic succession and a valid Eucharist. This in turn also injures the Catholic Church, called by the Lord to become for all *"one flock"* with *"one shepherd,"*[77] in that it hinders the complete fulfillment of its universality in history.

18. This situation seriously calls for ecumenical commitment on the part of everyone, with a view to achieving full communion in the unity of the Church; that unity *"which Christ bestowed on his Church from the beginning. This unity, we believe, subsists in the Catholic Church as something she can never lose, and we hope that it will continue to increase until the end of time."*[78] In this ecumenical commitment, important priorities are prayer, penance, study, dialogue and collaboration, so that, through a new conversion to the Lord, all may be enabled to recognize the continuity of the Primacy of Peter in his successors, the Bishops of Rome, and to see the Petrine ministry fulfilled, in the manner intended by the Lord, as a worldwide apostolic service, which is present in all the Churches *from within*, and which, while preserving its substance as a divine institution, can find expression in various ways according to the different circumstances of time and place, as history has shown.

Conclusion

19. The Blessed Virgin Mary is the model of ecclesial communion in faith, in charity and in union with Christ.[79] *"Eternally present in the mystery of Christ,"*[80] She is, in the midst of the Apostles, at the very heart of the Church at its birth[81] and of the Church of all ages. Indeed, *"the Church was congregated in the upper part (of the Cenacle) with Mary, who was the Mother of Jesus, and with his brethren. We cannot therefore speak of the Church unless Mary, the mother of the Lord, is present there, with the Lord's brethren."*[82]

---

77 Jn 10:16.
78 Decree *Unitatis Redintegratio*, no. 4/c.
79 Cf. Constitution *Lumen Gentium*, nos. 63 and 68; St. Ambrose, *Exposit. in Luc.*, 2, 7: PL 15, 1555; St. Isaac of Stella, *Sermo* 27: PL 194, 1778-1779; Rupert of Deutz, *De Vict. Verbi Dei*, 12, 1: PL 169, 1464-1465.
80 John Paul II, Encyclical *Redemptoris Mater*, 25-III-1987, no. 19.
81 Cf. Acts 1:14; John Paul II, Encyclical *Redemptoris Mater*: as quoted, no. 26.
82 St. Cromatius of Aquileia, *Sermo* 30, 1: "Sources Chrétiennes" 164, p. 134. Cf. Paul VI, Apostolic Exhortation *Marialis Cultus*, 2-II-1974, no. 28.

In bringing this *Letter* to a close, the Congregation for the Doctrine of the Faith, echoing the final words of the Constitution *Lumen Gentium*,[83] invites all the Bishops and, through them, all the faithful, especially the theologians, to entrust to the intercession of the Blessed Virgin their commitment to communion and to theological reflection upon communion.

The Sovereign Pontiff John Paul II, at the Audience granted to the undersigned Cardinal Prefect, approved this Letter, agreed upon in the ordinary meeting of this Congregation, and ordered its publication.
Rome, *at the Congregation for the Doctrine of the Faith, May 28, 1992.*

Joseph Card. Ratzinger
Prefect

✠ Alberto Bovone
Tit. Abp. of Caesarea in Numidia
Secretary

---

83 Cf. Constitution *Lumen Gentium*, no. 69.

COMMENTARIES AND STUDIES

The Church as Communion

Stanislao Nagy, SCI

I

The problem of the Church has interested Christian theological thought from the very beginning. The Gospel of St. Matthew, the captivity letters of St. Paul, the patristic ecclesiology represented by St. Irenaeus, St. Cyprian, and St. Augustine, the scholasticism of Gregory VII, Boniface VIII, Innocent III, the Reformation period as expressed in the ecclesiological thought of Robert Bellarmine and Stanislaus Osius, and, lastly, the modern period bracketed by the last two Councils present an impressive panorama of Christian fascination with the content of the mystery of the Church. The high point of this fascination has undoubtedly been reached in recent times. Beginning with the profoundly inspiring ecclesiological intuitions of J.A. Möhler, which resonated powerfully in Catholic reflection on the Church, it has born definitive and abundant fruits on the highest levels of the Church's Magisterium, both papal (Leo XIII, *Satis Cognitum*; Pius XII, *Mystici Corporis*; Paul VI, *Ecclesiam Suam*) and conciliar (the Constitutions of Vatican I, *Pastor Aeternus*, and of Vatican II, *Lumen Gentium* and *Gaudium et Spes*). The view of the truth about the Church expressed by the Constitution *Lumen Gentium* might have seemed to be the last word in theological reflection on the matter. A case in point is the prominence given to the category People of God in the Church's teaching, even though this did not exclude the possibility—indeed the necessity—of recourse to other categories such as Mystical Body, sacrament, or communion in reflection on the Church.

This state of affairs has been changing for a number of years, and, particularly since the Second Extraordinary Synod of Bishops, there is an increasing tendency to reevaluate the specifically ecclesiological character of the category *communio*. The final report of the Second Extraordinary Assembly of the Synod of Bishops asserted, "The ecclesiology of communion is the central and fundamental idea in the Council's documents," adding that "much was done by the Second Vatican Council so that the Church as communion might be more clearly understood and concretely incorporated into life."

While such strong language gave rise to some surprise when compared with the position of the Council expressed in the second chapter of the Constitution *Lumen Gentium*, it could not fail to elicit real consequences for reflection on the Church. It quickly became clear that this reflection had reached another level in its secular journey with the discovery that communion as a category enriched a deeper vision of the reality of the Church. There was no shortage of simplifications however, nor even of more or less conscious distortions, which served almost as a natural margin for this extraordinary intellectual fascination with such an important element of Christian truth. In the case of the category *communio*, the potential for misunderstanding and for a simplistic approach had already surfaced during the Council itself. A clear sign of this is the famous "*Nota praevia*" attached to the Constitution *Lumen Gentium*, which suggests an exact way of conceiving *communio* with regard to the reality of the Church.

In the current stage of ecclesiological studies, it is mainly two tendencies that cause concern: one that threatens what is specifically Christian about the content of *communio* and another that tends toward isolating it from other ecclesial categories, such as People of God, Mystical Body, and sacrament. In such a situation there is clearly a need for competent guidance to help prevent potential distortion or even mere impoverishment of this important thread in Catholic ecclesiological thought: the Church as seen through the perspective of the category *communio*.

II

The more remote semantic origins of the concept of *communio* do not derive from Christianity. The term *koinonía* was borrowed from the Greek world, where it stood for an interpersonal bond based on a value held in common. In its secular understanding, defined by the elements of a common gift and the personal relationships created thereby, it held out a particularly valuable potential for Christianity.

At the same time, however, doubts were raised about whether this original meaning could adequately express a special Christian content. In fact, both the phenomenon of a commonly held value and the reality of the relationships arising from it invest Christian *koinonía* with a meaning so rich and multifaceted that the poor and simple signifying powers of secular *koinonía* are incapable of embracing or expressing it.

In such a situation, the meaning of the secular archetype was very quickly changed, assuming a clear, categorically Christian profile with a growing tendency toward various new applications. Employment of the category *communio* therefore demands a certain caution in describing the semantic range of the secular prototype and likewise a continual effort to establish the deep biblical and patristic roots revealed in the specifically Christian use of the term. Minimizing, or worse yet, ignoring what is different and specific about Christian communion exposes this term to the danger of being partially or even falsely understood and employed. An eloquent example of such a danger is offered by the conviction expressed every now and again that the category of *communio* is a tool applicable to various sectors of life, even of Christian life, which can be used as a special key capable of resolving everything.

In the Christian understanding, based above all on the inspiration deriving from the New Testament, communion is referenced in various contexts in Christian doctrine and life; for example, the mystery of the Holy Trinity or the entire question of sanctity considered at the ontological or dynamic-practical level. The Magisterium of the Council, which uses the term 112 times, is an eloquent example and instructive illustration.

There is no doubt, however, that the central connotation of this concept in Catholic theological reflection, theoretical and practical, both during the Council and in its aftermath, is the mystery of the Church. This is undoubtedly and primarily thanks to its particular adaptability and its ability to express and clarify the richness of the truth about the Church by means of its two basic elements, which are the source and the consequences of her communitarian structure.

III

The point of departure for the essence of *communio* lies in the value around which people are gathered. It is precisely this value that provides the source and determines the quality of the relationships among the members of the community.

In the case of the *communio* of the Church, this basic structural element surpasses all the values that come into play at the level of natural communities. The values that constitute the ecclesial *communio* are, generally speaking, supernatural. Thus, their origin lies in the supernatural economy of grace; that is, at a level decidedly higher than that of natural human existence. On the other hand, the deepest source of this ontological diversity of the order of grace lies in man's original destiny to the dignity of God's son, which is superior to his natural state. *Lumen Gentium* expresses it concisely, speaking about the eternal plan of salvation: "The eternal Father . . . created the whole world. His plan was to dignify men with a participation in His own divine life" (no. 2). The same constitution further concretizes the divine plan that ennobles man from his very origins by presenting the infinite richness of ways in which it is realized: "All the elect, before time began, the Father 'foreknew and predestined to become conformed to the image of his Son, that he should be the firstborn among many brethren'" (*Lumen Gentium*, no. 2). It should be noted that *Lumen Gentium* cites the inspired words of the Letter to the Romans (8:29) in making this affirmation, so as to guarantee its certainty and to accentuate its importance all the more. For the exceptional quality of the prospect of man's divinization gains further sublimity in the surprising economy that brings it about: this economy could be expressed in brief as "sonship in the Son." So it is possible—indeed necessary—to speak about a particular density of ontological richness of the economy of man's salvation, a density that is further completed by the powerfully articulated mystery of the infinite love of God, eloquently expressed in St. Paul's summary affirmation: "Christ loved us and handed himself over" (Eph 5:2).

The *communio* of the Church contains this entire infinite richness of the mystery of salvation, which implies the involvement of the Holy Trinity. It is contained as the fundamental, defining element of its divine-human reality and as the precious treasure of the grace of salvation of which it is trustee and dispenser. The Council had clearly expounded this in the *Decree on Ecumenism* when it asserted, "What has revealed the love of God among us is that the only-begotten Son of God has been sent by the Father into the world, so that, being made man, the Son might by His redemption of the entire human race give new life to it and unify it. . . . After being lifted up on the cross and glorified, the Lord Jesus poured forth the Spirit whom He had promised, and through whom He has called and gathered together the people of the New Covenant, who comprise the Church, into a unity of faith, hope, and charity" (*Unitatis Redintegratio*, no. 2). Likewise significant and not without notes of profound admiration is St. Paul's expression when, at the conclusion of the presentation of the plan of salvation realized in Christ, he says that God the Father "put all things beneath his feet and gave him as head over all things to the church, which is his body, the fullness of the one who fills all things in every way" (Eph 1:22-23).

It is precisely this fullness, this indescribable economy of salvation realized by the will of the Father through the Son in the Holy Spirit, that is the fundamental element of the Church-*communio*. On God's part, this element appears as infinite love; on the part of man and of humanity on the other hand, as an inexpressible gift of infinite value that decides human fate.

Deposited in the heart of the Church, this most precious treasure of the work of salvation produces a number of consequences, one of which makes itself particularly evident. It is the other component of the ecclesial *communio*, namely unity, which develops in two directions. First and foremost it constitutes a profound, inexpressible bond between God—the giver of the gift of salvation—and man, who is its designated recipient. The nucleus of this bond is the dignity of being an adopted son of God, the divine filiation in Christ of the members of the Church-*communio*. The issue here is the unimaginably profound unity in the orientation of the transcendent God and the limited human being.

This foundational link, the consequence of the presence of the economy of salvation in the Church, has a particular equivalent on the horizontal level in the relationship among the members of the Church. The dignity of Son of God in Christ that they enjoy relates them to each other as brothers. These brothers are united not only by the supernatural consanguinity that flows from the grace of salvation but also by membership in the "holy People of God" (*Lumen Gentium*, no. 12), the new humanity, the new family of God.

IV

The deep bonds between God, who effects this salvation in the Church, and those who participate in it, like the ties that bind these participants to each other, are not the only coefficients of the ecclesial *communio*. Another essential component, connected with *communio* and with the structure of the Church, lies in the economy of the sacraments. The Church, in and of itself, is already as sacrament, a great transmitter of salvific values and of the divine-human and interpersonal bonds flowing from them that she holds in her heart. Beginning from this symbolic mission, however, her operative-instrumental participation in the process of transmitting the grace of salvation to the human person who needs it is inscribed into the very structure of the Church. The *Constitution on the Church* expresses it in this way: "Established by Christ as a fellowship of life, charity, and truth, it is also used by Him as an instrument for the redemption of all, and is sent forth into the whole world as the light of the world and the salt of the earth (cf. Mt 5:12-16)" (*Lumen Gentium*, no. 9).

This fundamental sacramentality of the Church-*communio* is realized in the economy of the sacraments at work in her. The sacraments are effective means of grace in the sphere of human life. The key role played by the economy of the sacraments in the life of the Church-*communio* is clearly shown by the decisive importance of baptism in the process of her foundation and in the way in which she functions. *Lumen Gentium* affirms, "Incorporated into the Church through baptism . . . reborn as sons of God, they must confess before men the faith which they have received from God through the Church" (no. 11), and adds that in the community of the Church so understood, "the life of Christ is poured into the believers, who, through the sacraments, are united . . . to Christ who suffered and was glorified" (no. 7).

The sacramentality so clearly impressed on the structure of the Church's communion is essentially connected to one additional element, her visibility and invisibility. The deepest sense of sacramentality lies in the coexistence of the invisible and supernatural world of grace with the visible and created sign that remains in a specific relationship with the world of grace. In the case of the Church-*communio*, the expression of this double level is the invisibility of the supernatural mystery of man's communion with God and the visibility of the Church's hierarchical structure, which is linked to the presence and operation of the triple mission of Christ-Messiah in her.

The sacrament of the Eucharist is situated at the very heart of the Church-*communio*, both under the aspect of the salvific sacrifice of Christ truly present there and in terms of the supernatural nourishment that Christ makes of himself in Holy Communion. Both dimensions of this sacrament bring the mystery of the saving presence of God the Savior into the context of the community of the faithful in the Church, becoming the revelation of this presence to the world and, within the Church itself, the source and summit of ecclesial community. *Lumen Gentium* asserts that "truly partaking of the body of the Lord in the breaking of the Eucharistic bread, we are taken up into communion with Him and with one another. 'Because the bread is one, we though many, are one body, all of us who partake of the one bread' (1 Cor 10:17). In this way all of us are made members of His body (1 Cor 12:27) 'but severally members one of another'" (no.7). The final two passages of this quote, taken from the letters of St. Paul, demonstrate the central role of the Eucharist in the process of forming the Church-*communio*: "We are made members of His Body," the Body of Christ the Savior and "severally members one of another," united by the invisible bonds of participation in His life (cf. *Lumen Gentium*, no. 7).

The bond among the members of the Church-*communio*, realized with particular power in the mystery of the Eucharist, possesses more than the earthly, temporal dimension associated with the Church considered in terms of its earthly, historical existence. This bond exists no less powerfully in the eschatological dimension, making the inseparable connection between the

Church militant on earth with the Church suffering and triumphant that is already in the realm of the ultimate realization in eternity.

This fact stretches the limits of the *communio* of the Church indefinitely, joining those who have already reached the fullness of the life in Christ and already enjoy the possession of God together with those who are on the path that leads safely and surely to that end. This is accomplished on the basis of communal possession of Christ's life of grace in the Holy Spirit. The union so created is, in effect, organic in nature, and it makes this union a vital and supportive bond in supernatural charity. It comprises not only the objective albeit invisible state of togetherness but also the state of permanent, supernatural, reciprocal openness (*communio*) in the form of a specific exchange of gifts. For those who are already in eternity, it expresses itself as intercession on behalf of those still making the earthly pilgrimage; for these latter, it manifests itself in veneration of those who have already reached the goal of salvation in Christ and through Christ.

The summit, the thing that holds together this communion of the Church in pilgrimage through time and living in the glory of eternity, is the liturgical mystery whose lynchpin is the Eucharistic sacrifice. Through this sacrifice, as *Lumen Gentium* says, "we are most closely united to the worshiping Church in heaven as we join with and venerate the memory first of all of the glorious ever-Virgin Mary, of Blessed Joseph and the blessed apostles and martyrs, and of all the saints" (no. 50).

The foregoing considerations of the content of *communio* as a category referring to the reality of the Church as described in the *Letter* published by the Congregation for the Doctrine of the Faith have attempted to uncover a mere fragment of the truth to be discovered from this perspective. It is, however, a fragment of the immense richness of truth. If we begin from a proper understanding of *communio* and avoid the distortions that can get in the way, there are many other components that contribute to a better understanding of the reality of the Church, so that on earth she may really be and always remain the "light of the nations."

Universal Church and Particular Churches

ANTONIO MARIA SICARI, ODC

"God save us from confusing the routine of our mental habits with divine Truth!"

Henri de Lubac's reflection-invocation (in *More Paradoxes*) is especially necessary when we deal with the "mystery of the Church" because of the many positions and points of tension that surround it.

But the mind is filled with habits even before entering into the sacred precinct.

The sociological concepts and experiences in which we are immersed often work in a reductive sense that limits our perspective so that the dimensions of the mystery become diminished or distorted.

At other times contemporary ideas exert a one-sided effect: caught up in the passion of exalting (or condemning) some particular detail, they end up dismembering the whole with no concern that everything might become unhinged and unstable.

This is what has happened to many who have been concerned with redefining more exactly the relationships that should exist between the universal Church and the particular Churches: "mental habits" took certain expressions of Vatican II and bent them to predetermined interpretations.

Admittedly, the expression of *Lumen Gentium* was stimulating and confident when it referred to "particular church[es], fashioned after the model of the universal Church. In and from such individual churches [*in quibus et ex quibus*] there comes into being the one and only Catholic Church" (no. 23).

So there was a desire to respond to a certain theological and pastoral imbalance in the past that certainly needed to be recognized: the risk of confusing universalism with centralism and of making the universal Church coincide with the Church of Rome; the risk that particular Churches might be understood as "branch offices" or "provinces" or "parts" of the universal Church.

There was even more desire to promote a new sense of ecumenical and missionary communion: to restore to the particular Churches the full awareness that in them "the one, holy, catholic, and apostolic Church of Christ is truly present and operative" (*Christus Dominus*, no. 11); to connect them among themselves and with the Church of Rome on the strength of their very nature; to demonstrate that the inextricable and fertile root of this communion lies in the Eucharist and in the collegial union of the bishops (*cum Petro et sub Petro*).

But this confident expression (*in quibus et ex quibus una et unica Ecclesia catholica existit*) was destined to become very easy prey to mental habits that were already widespread and ingrained.

Some began to talk of the relative primacy of the particular Churches; then the relative became more and more absolute until the universal Church risked being seen as the mere sum of a mutual federation of Churches.

The more attentive certainly continued to demand that particular Churches have the necessary elements to be true churches (at least insisting on the presence of a true Successor of the Apostles and on the celebration of a true Eucharist).

Everything else was not negated but left unsaid, and the other part of the conciliar doctrine—according to which the "particular Churches (are) fashioned after the model of the universal Church"—suffered a paradoxical fate. Many came to consider the universal Church as a model.

Some pushed further still, using the fateful formula "*in quibus et ex quibus*" as a pretext for rethinking the very origin of the Church and of its powers: generated not by Christ but by agreement among those who gathered in his name.

As always, what was needed was fidelity to that "catholic conjunction" (*et . . . et*) which alone guarantees and shows the way toward a humble approach to the mystery, the refusal to be sidetracked by mental habits, the desire to safeguard the received gift in its entirety.

The recent Letter of the Congregation for the Doctrine of the Faith *On Some Aspects of the Church Understood as Communion* effects this integration decisively in number 9: "The formula of the Second Vatican Council: *The Church in and formed out of the Churches* (*Ecclesia in et ex Ecclesiis*), is inseparable from this other formula: *The Churches in and formed out of the Church* (*Ecclesiae in et ex Ecclesia*).'"

The particular Churches, therefore, represent the flowering of the universal Church here and now without reducing it to an abstraction.

If it were not for the universal Church giving birth to the particular Churches—maternally prior both historically and ontologically—these churches would be even less than an abstraction; they would be a lie.

"The unity of the particular Churches," de Lubac sagely taught, "should reflect the unity that held among the Apostles."

We must constantly return to these first moments of Church history, when the universal Church was visibly expressed and formed in and from those who were about to become founders of Churches.

At that time, however, it would never have occurred to any of these men to consider themselves as an "origin" since it was so obvious who the Origin was who had established them as one single whole.

Basically, what our mental habits must never contaminate is precisely this all-embracing mystery that we call "communion."

Communion is God in the intimacy of his Trinitarian life.

Communion is the model according to which God has imagined and created men (both in the relationship of each individual with him and in the social relations that they must recognize and live out among themselves).

Communion is the gift of Christ: from his entry into humanity, to the sacrifice that he has offered *pro nobis*, to the salvific and glorious attraction of the risen body, to the outpouring of his one and only Spirit upon his disciples and on all of creation.

Communion is the Eucharist in which the gift and the Giver are communicated in their entirety.

Communion is the power that binds individual believers to Christ (when they participate in his holy gifts) and to each other.

Communion is the power that enables the universal Church to give birth to the individual particular Churches while keeping them in her bosom.

Communion is the link that binds the individual particular Churches to each other, especially by creating orderly mutual bonds among their shepherds through the bond that links each of them with the Bishop of Rome.

Communion is the goal and the task of every ministry and every gift that the Spirit gives to the churches to allow them to live as a single body, properly coordinated and connected.

Communion is the relationship that unites the Church (and the churches) of yesteryear with those of today and those of tomorrow, keeping generation after generation of the faithful immersed in a single vital stream.

Communion is the sustaining link that unites the pilgrim Church with the heavenly Church.

Communion is that dynamism that sets all these realities in relation and in motion and points them toward their mission: the conversion of the entire world.

And finally, Communion can properly be called "the Eucharist received," which makes the individual Christian a full participant, here and now, of infinite riches.

The word, which must certainly be taken analogically, remains the same and is always true and absolutely unequivocal.

The repeated use of the same word, conscious that it is being applied analogically, helps express the mutual interiority of its individual aspects.

Some theologians rightly speak of "reciprocal immanence of the defining elements," which must never become disconnected.

It is safe to say that, somewhere along the course of analogy, error crept in with the failure to see how one element or one aspect of such a rich communion requires the other and benefits from the connection.

The life of the universal Church and of the particular Churches is saturated with one and the same mystery of communion.

On the strength of such a communal mystery, the universal Church always makes herself "present and active amid the particular characteristics and the diversity of persons, groups, times and places," and, when it presents all the essential elements, even the particular merits the name of Church (cf. no. 7).

Therefore, only the right relationship between the universal Church and the particular Churches can guarantee the benefits that are essential for the faithful.

The document of the Congregation for the Doctrine of the Faith explicitly mentions at least two of these.

First and foremost is the benefit of the Church's freedom. A particular Church that weakens its link with the universal Church does not become self-sufficient but rather fragile in itself and risks "losing its own freedom in the face of the various forces of slavery and exploitation" (no. 8). What is striking today in so many inter-ecclesial assertions of autonomy and in so many expressions of the anti-Roman complex is not so much the inconsistency of the theological principles invoked but the historical blindness, the failure to have learned what history has continually documented and continues to document.

If it is true that the close (and juridical) bonds between the universal Church and the particular Churches can occasionally engender some degree of overbearance due to human weakness, it is even more true that to the degree these bonds are relaxed, other, more pernicious dependencies will always be established.

Whatever is particular will always be the historical expression of the presence and action of something that is universal; it will either be the Church or it will be the world. A particular Church never becomes self-sufficient; it becomes worldly.

The other aspect to be highlighted regards the *freedom of every Christian*.

The individual believer is particular, and nonetheless—paradoxically—nothing particular will suffice for him; he requires the communion that is by its very nature universal.

Thus, the right relationship between particular Churches and the universal Church guarantees his freedom.

It is worth the trouble to list here the consequences specified by the Congregation's document (cf. no. 10), because they respond to more than a few questions and discomforts that have troubled Christians ever since the imposition of a strict interpretation of that "primacy of the local Church" to which we have already alluded.

- The Christian enters the Church by means of the particular but he belongs "in an immediate way" to the universal Church.
- He can never be considered a stranger in any Church even though he belongs to a particular Church.
- And everywhere, especially in the celebration of the Eucharist, "he finds himself in his Church."

Admittedly, these declarations were really needed, as were those expressed in number 16: "There are institutions and communities . . . [that] belong *as such* to the universal Church, though their members are also members of the particular Churches where they live and work."

The document recalled especially those ecclesial realities which, "given their supradiocesan character, rooted in the Petrine ministry . . . are also elements at the service of communion among the various particular Churches" (no. 16).

This is one more proof, as if one were still required, that the need for real freedom in the Church is always felt and guaranteed more by one who has responsibility for the universal Church than by all those who would like to guarantee it to the particular Churches and within them—at the price of a new peripheral centralism.

Essentially, it would suffice to keep two simple truths before our eyes and in our hearts as we approach the mystery of the Church.

The first: in the Church, the correct relationship between universal and particular is not realized when the universal recedes before the particular but when the particular opens itself to the universal and lets itself be drawn to it and enhanced by it.

The second: in the Church the value of the particular does not come from opposing the universal but rather because it represents the generous point of arrival, here and now, of a universal mission.

Communion of the Churches, Eucharist and Episcopacy

Louis Bouyer of the Oratory

Of late both the faithful and their pastors have given renewed attention to the fact that the manifestation, or better, the fundamental realization of the universal Church takes place in every Eucharistic celebration. Effectively, wherever the Eucharist is celebrated, there the Church is, and not merely that part of the Catholic Church defined by every local church, but the Church whole and entire, indivisible in its unity.

In fact, it is fair to say that what produced the Church at its origins and preserves it on earth throughout the centuries is primarily the fact that Christians receive in it the whole fundamental proclamation of the divine Word; that they receive it along with the prayer of faith; that they witness the elements of their life that they have presented, the bread and wine, consecrated as the body and blood of their divine Head, which they receive all together so as to share in the very act of salvation, renewing and nourishing the initial identification with the Savior himself deriving from their baptism. In this way, the Church manifests and ceaselessly develops its own reality.

As John of St. Thomas says in a phrase that could be called inspired, our Lord, by consecrating the first Eucharist at the Last Supper eaten together with his Apostles on the night before his death on the Cross, foresaw and consecrated in advance, by means of the Apostles and the bishops who succeeded them (along with the priests of the second order who collaborate with them) all the Eucharists that would be celebrated until the end of time.

For the same reason, by taking part in a "legitimate" (as Tertullian says) Eucharistic celebration, we communicate with the whole body of the faithful called to make up the total body of Christ—according to the expression of St. Augustine—through our own communion with the act of salvific love: the reconciling Cross, the down-payment and anticipation of the Mass of the general resurrection on the last day.

This presumes, of course, that just as the apostolic college operated inseparably in every crucial action of each of its members inasmuch as it represented, in a real and not artificial way, the only One who sent them out all together, so too, each bishop (or every priest representing him in the celebration of the Eucharist) acts only by virtue of this representative share in the one, definitive priesthood of Christ himself. Therefore, all the local Eucharists until the parousia are nothing but a single celebration in which the Paschal Christ remains the consecrator and, as such, these celebrations gather and unite all the faithful of all times, wherever they gather, in one single communion.

But this implies that, in every diocese, each priest of the second order merely extends the Eucharist celebrated by the bishop into each local community. By the same token, the celebration of each bishop, one in source and in foundation with all his confreres in the episcopacy, prolongs that primordial celebration in which Christ joined the Twelve to himself in a unique way, making it fully real throughout the whole world and over the course of the centuries.

Thus, all the Masses of all times in all places extend and prolong the one Eucharist of the one Savior and reconciler of a humanity redeemed and reconciled in one single Church.

In the same way, the entire Catholic Church of today, united—or rather one—with the Church of centuries past, and anticipating the Second Coming, which will crown the ultimate Eucharistic celebration, reveals itself and is made present in the reciprocal communion of all those who, whether in the past or today, throughout the earth or already in heaven, continue the one celebration of the very first Mass or make it eternal in the worship of the sacrificed but glorious Lamb revealed to the seer of the Apocalypse.

In every place where a legitimate Eucharist is celebrated it is, therefore, the local bishop, successor to the Apostles, who actualizes, whether personally or through the priests of the second order who are an extension of his priesthood, the communion of all with each other and with the sole Head of his own body, which never ceases to extend itself in all its members as they continue to multiply.

However, since the local communion is affirmed and made real in the celebration of the local bishop, it is no less essential that these local communities should be epiphanies, multiple manifestations of the universal Church over which the Church of Rome, the Church of Peter, "presides in charity," as the martyr St. Ignatius says.

In fact, it was a characteristic of the very creation of the apostolic college by Christ—even Protestant exegetes like Oscar Cullman admit it, although they hesitate to recognize how the college of bishops succeeds it—that what is conferred collectively on the Twelve inseparably is also conferred individually on Peter inasmuch as he is invested with a personal responsibility for the unity of this body.

It follows from this perspective that there is no need to choose (as has often happened in the polemics between Eastern Orthodox and Catholics) between the personal mission of Peter and the collective mission of the apostolic college from which Peter is inseparable just as this college is inseparable from him. For just as during his earthly life, Christ has willed to be present not only with us all but in us all, with a presence that remains essentially personal even though it is common to all. This effectively proves that one of the Trinity, the Son who has made himself one of us, will not simply be like a new Adam for a renewed human nature but, as St. Paul says, "Adam, the last man," the total man in whom we are all recapitulated and reconciled forever.

From this perspective, what is essential to every manifestation or rather local realization of the Church, especially in the celebration of the Eucharist, is that everyone should act in harmony through the ministry of a single individual, the representative of the properly apostolic grace of the sole Head, from whom the one Spirit is poured out into the hearts of all.

Just as in the Eucharist the consecration of the gifts and communion of all follows from the authoritative announcement by the successor of the Apostles or one of his collaborators in the priesthood of the evangelical Word received with faith, so too, in each local Church, everyone is called to live the same faith that awakens and enlivens the apostolic preaching in them all. In the same manner, in the universal Church, the Successor of Peter is like the sacramental sign of Catholic unity in the faith of the one Church whole and entire.

According to this same view, the pastor in the local Church who is in communion with the episcopacy as a whole is especially in communion with the pastor responsible for the unity of all. Finally, by renewing themselves in the unity of such a communion each time they offer in common the basic foods of their very existence, the bread and wine presented for irradiation by the divine Word recalled by the apostolic prayer, everyone can communicate in their turn in the one Body of the one Christ. Thus everyone, in every place until this very moment, can say: "I live, no longer I, but Christ lives in me." This affirmation will also apply inseparably to each believer in particular and to the one Church extending to every place. By remaining part of this Church and actively sharing in all its gifts, every Christian is a Christian in the indivisible unity of this apostolic Church, in the communion of the apostolic body and in the communion of the body of Christ himself, "who presides in charity."

Unity and Diversity in Ecclesial Communion

FERNANDO OCÁRIZ

"The universality of the Church involves, on the one hand, a most solid unity, and on the other, a *plurality* and a *diversification*, which do not obstruct unity, but rather confer upon it the character of 'communion.'" These words of John Paul II begin the fourth part (nos. 15-16) of the recent *Letter to the Bishops of the Catholic Church on Some Aspects of the Church Understood as Communion*. The *Letter* relates the plurality and diversification that confer the character of communion on unity "both to the diversity of ministries, charisms, and forms of life and apostolate within each particular Church, and to the diversity of traditions in liturgy and culture among the various particular Churches" (no. 15).

The *Letter* does not view the relationship between unity and diversity in terms of dialectical tension; it is not, in fact, a matter of unity in spite of diversity nor of diversity in spite of unity. In the mystery of the Church, unity and diversity are two foundational dimensions of communion. In a way, communion could be said to offer us a notion that synthesizes the four marks of the Church. This is obvious, first and foremost, regarding unity and catholicity (universality) but likewise regarding apostolicity and holiness. Apostolicity, because ecclesial communion is also communion with the Church of all times and places, which, by means of the apostolic succession, is the same Church founded upon Peter and the other Apostles (cf. no. 12). Holiness, not merely because the Church is the Communion of Saints, but also and most importantly because the ultimate root of unity and diversity is the Holy Spirit, who fills and unites the whole Church while distributing over her a great variety of gifts (cf. no. 6). For this same reason, "the concept of *communion* lies 'at the heart of the Church's self-understanding'" (no. 3). As a synthesis of unity, holiness, catholicity, and apostolicity, communion also assumes a particular pastoral importance inasmuch as it stipulates that one of the fundamental tasks of the Roman Pontiff in the universal Church and of the bishop in the particular Church is the promotion of diversification as well as of unity (cf. no. 15).

There is more to this aspect of ecclesial communion than unity in diversity among the particular Churches and the existence within each of these Churches of diverse forms of life and apostolate deriving from the legitimate freedom of individuals and from particular charisms. In fact, the *Letter* affirms that, in this context, "one needs to bear in mind that there are institutions and communities established by the Apostolic Authority for specific pastoral tasks. They belong *as such* to the universal Church, though their members are also members of the particular Churches where they live and work" (no. 16). Thus, they are particular expressions of the universal Church in the particular Churches that are not mutually reducible to each other in an exclusive manner. The tenor of this passage makes it obvious that the *Letter* is referring to personal prelatures for specific pastoral tasks and to other institutions established by the Apostolic Authority for the pastoral care of particular groups of the faithful belonging to different particular Churches, as is the case with military ordinariates. The simultaneous membership of members of the faithful in these institutions and in particular Churches "takes different juridical forms" (no. 16), but in every case "it does not erode the unity of the particular Church founded on the Bishop; rather, it helps endow this unity with the interior diversification which is a feature of *communion*" (no. 16).

In the context of unity and diversity in ecclesial communion, the *Letter* also considers the many institutions of consecrated life and societies of apostolic life "with which the Holy Spirit enriches the Mystical Body of Christ. Although these do not belong to the hierarchical structure of the Church, they belong to its life and holiness" (no. 16). The *Letter* adds no further clarifications about how these institutions and societies are integrated into the universal Church and the particular Churches, perhaps because these aspects are already quite clear and require no explanation. Neither is any explicit reference made to other important ecclesial realities arising out of initiatives by the faithful (associations, movements, etc.), which are also expressions of unity and diversity in ecclesial communion. The requirement of unity around the bishop (to use the traditional phrase) likewise applies to them: a unity around the bishop that does not limit diversification but, on the contrary, guarantees it and makes it truly ecclesial.

By highlighting the variety of institutions at work in a particular Church, the *Letter* draws attention to its *catholic density*. For such a variety manifests that the one Church of Christ is truly present and operative in the particular Church, so that the life of the particular Church is a true image of the universal Church.

The remarkable doctrinal depth of the *Letter* is likewise made evident in the clarity with which it manages to express the fact that the necessary character of a particular Church (which is to say that entrance into and life in the universal Church are necessarily accomplished in a particular Church; cf. no. 10) is not in the least opposed to the recognition and promotion of every legitimate diversification. This rules out, among other things, the risk of ecclesial impoverishment that the conception of unity as uniformity would represent.

Equally worth noting is how the *Letter* first recalls that building up and safeguarding the unity to which diversification confers the character of communion is the primordial responsibility of the pope and the bishops, and then adds that this is "also a task of everyone in the Church, because all are called to build it up and preserve it each day, above all by means of that charity which is '*the bond of perfection*' (Col 3:14)" (no. 15). Clearly this is not a pious thought without ecclesiological relevance; in fact, the *Letter* uses these words to express a fundamental ecclesial requirement. Especially after Vatican II, there has been much reflection in the field of ecumenism on the scandal represented by division among Christians and on the obstacle this division raises for the work of evangelization. This should also be stated, perhaps even more forcefully, in the face of divisions within the Catholic Church itself. Diversification is not division, nor is the legitimate autonomy of persons and institutions. It is rather the absence of "that charity which is the bond of perfection" that would be radically divisive, an absence already evident in "rivalry, jealousy, fury, selfishness, slander, gossip, conceit, and disorder" (2 Cor 12:20) in some early Christian communities. On the contrary, charity, which is the spiritual root of communion and in which we must all make constant progress in the Holy Spirit, includes respect and understanding of others and extends as far as profound joy for the success of others in preaching Christ (cf. Phil 1:18).

In conclusion then, the *Letter* also serves as encouragement to promote a renewed way of imagining and living an ecclesial communion in which the primacy of God's gifts is resplendent even in the unavoidable dimensions of organization and administration.

Ecclesial Communion and Ecumenism

MAX THURIAN

Ecumenism is the search for visible unity among baptized Christians "who openly confess Jesus Christ as God and Lord and as the sole Mediator between God and man unto the glory of the one God, Father, Son, and Holy Spirit" (*Unitatis Redintegratio*, no. 20). These Christians, separated from the Catholic Church gathered together by the ministry of the Bishop of Rome, either have not maintained full communion with the Successor of Peter (the Orthodox) or have not preserved the entire Catholic doctrine inherited from the faith of the Apostles (the Protestants). Thanks to numerous common elements of the faith and the Church of Christ, we can still recognize with joy and hope a certain communion, albeit imperfect, between these separated Christians and the Catholic Church (*Unitatis Redintegratio*, no. 8; *Lumen Gentium*, no. 15).

The Catholic Church recognizes that it is very closely united to the Eastern Orthodox Churches, since they have preserved the apostolic succession and the triple ministry of the episcopacy, priesthood, and diaconate, not to mention the fullness of the celebration of the Eucharist (*Letter*, no. 17). In a real way, the Church of God is built up and grows through the celebration of the Lord's Eucharist in these particular Churches (*Unitatis Redintegratio*, no. 15). Even though they are separated from the See of Peter, they are particular Churches or sister churches, in which the one, holy, catholic, and apostolic Church is truly present.

Communion with the universal Church represented by the Successor of Peter is not an external complement to the existence of a particular Church but rather is part of its internal structure. Hence, the separation of the Eastern Orthodox Churches from the Roman See of Peter constitutes a wound in their condition as particular Churches. Still, the Catholic Church has a great responsibility toward these churches to help them in carrying out their ministry of evangelization and edification. Such assistance is especially important today in Eastern Europe.

The wound is deeper in ecclesial communities that have not maintained the apostolic succession or preserved the full celebration of the Eucharist.

Protestants manifest another way of being Christian in exclusive obedience to Sacred Scripture but without the continuity of the apostolic Tradition or the sacramental fullness of the Eucharist, which, for the Catholic Church, are fundamental and defining elements of the Church.

Division among Christians injures the Catholic Church as well, inasmuch as it stands in the way of fully realizing her universality in history (*Letter*, no. 17). Nevertheless, the Catholic Church believes that the unity conferred by Christ subsists in her and that she cannot lose it, and she hopes that this unity will grow day after day (*Unitatis Redintegratio*, no. 4). The efforts of ecumenism seek full communion in the unity conferred on the Church by Christ from the very beginning (*Letter*, no. 18).

The unity sought by the ecumenical movement is not a fusion of churches that would suppress all legitimate diversity for the sake of a single concept of Christian community. True ecumenism does not seek unity in uniformity to the detriment of the richness of the Spirit's gifts, which the Church needs in order to respond to the manifold mission Christ has entrusted to her.

Neither, however, can it be limited to a fraternal coexistence that would permit every form of faith, of worship, and of behavior, so long as it was inspired by a liberal interpretation of the Gospel. Such an attitude is based on faith in an invisible Church that unites all Christians irrespective of the institution to which they belong.

Another attitude contents itself with a reconciled diversity on the level of faith and ecclesial institutions. Faced with considerable difficulty in reaching theological or ecclesiological agreements, it would be better, according to this line of thought, to recognize the diversity of positions, accept them, and even justify them, seeking reconciliation on a spiritual level without requiring any visible unity.

Thus, the possibility of a sort of federative contract has been imagined, whereby the churches would be recognized just as they are, the preservation of their identity would be justified on the basis of the diversity of gifts that lie at the origin of their existence, and their particular mission would continue in fidelity to the original form that characterizes them. The churches could form a sort of federation, with each preserving its own emphases in matters of belief and the specific structures of its organization.

The true ecumenical attitude that opens a path toward the visible unity of Christians and of the churches is the one described by the Second Vatican Council: interior conversion, renewal of the inner life, self-denial, sincere humility, gentle service, and fraternal generosity toward others. "There can be no ecumenism worthy of the name without a change of heart. For it is from newness of attitudes (cf. Eph 4:23), from self-denial and unstinted love, that yearnings for unity take their rise and grow toward maturity. We should therefore pray to the divine Spirit for the grace to be genuinely self-denying, humble, gentle in the service of others, and to have an attitude of brotherly generosity toward them" (*Unitatis Redintegratio*, no. 7).

The visible unity of Christians in the one Church willed by Christ consists in recognizing what is fundamental for the existence of a real communion of particular Churches in the universal Church. Ecumenical dialogues concluding with written statements of agreement in recent decades have sought this visible unity in what is necessary and fundamental. Today we are in a position to identify the points of agreement and the points of significant disagreement that will require effort to change mindsets if we wish to arrive at a fundamental, visible unity, the unity that is necessary and sufficient for a true communion of particular Churches and of ecclesial communities in the universal Church.

There is agreement on belief in a God who is both One and Trinity and in Christ true God and true Man; recognition of the unique and manifold Word of God transmitted by the Bible read within Tradition; reciprocal recognition of baptism, which is the entrance into the communion with Christ and with the Church; and, for many, the recognition of the basic faith expressed in the Creed of Nicaea-Constantinople. Yet disagreements still remain, which the statements of doctrinal agreement have not diminished.

The greatest steps forward in agreement on belief have been made with regard to the Eucharist. Admittedly, concelebration between Catholic and Protestant ministers is not possible because of disagreement over the nature of the ministerial priesthood. Still, an important rapprochement has been achieved on the theological level. The Eucharist is the memorial, that is, the actualization, of the sacrifice of Christ crucified and risen. The Eucharist is the presence of Christ who offers himself as food that is essential and vital to human beings. Catholic faith draws a strict connection between this real presence and the bread and wine that become by consecration the body and blood of Christ, the total person of the Crucified and Risen One. He offers himself as food and may be adored outside the celebration. Protestants hesitate over the conversion of ordinary bread and wine into the body and blood of Christ and do not believe that this real presence endures. This is a different view of the gift of God to his creature and of the irrevocable link created by the word of Christ and the power of the Holy Spirit in Eucharistic consecration.

Another point of disagreement that needs to be resolved is the concept of ministry, because the concelebration of the Eucharist depends on a reciprocal recognition of ministries. According to Catholic belief, ordination transmits the gifts of the Holy Spirit needed to exercise a permanent ecclesial function. This sacrament distinguishes among the People of God, on the basis of a particular character, those who are called to be ministers of Christ's priesthood. The recognition of ministers by the imposition of hands in Protestant communities does not establish an essential difference between pastors and laypeople, since the Supper can even be celebrated by a layperson delegated by the relevant authority.

The Catholic Church considers the continuity of the ecclesial body, assured from the very beginning through the structure of the episcopacy, to be essential. The bishop is the necessary minister of unity within the particular Church and of the unity between this church and the other particular Churches and with the pope. Continuity in time does not have a decisive importance for Protestant communions. For them, what is fundamental is obedience to Scripture alone. Protestants reject the role of the bishop as the minister of ecumenical communion and of historical continuity with the Apostles. The Catholic sacramental episcopacy, reaffirmed by Vatican II, is foreign to Protestant ecclesiology.

Moreover, as everyone knows, recognition of the universal ministry of unity exercised by the Bishop of Rome, the pope, divides Catholics and Protestants. Nevertheless, many ties of friendship have been established, and Pope John Paul II always desires to dialogue with non-Catholics during his apostolic travels. Many visits have been made by Protestant leaders to him in Rome. This is something new that could mark a milestone in the path toward unity, inasmuch as friendship among Christians is a necessary bridge in the construction of unity. The Catholic Church hopes that ecumenical conversion will allow everyone to recognize in the Bishop of Rome the sign and structure of the unity of the particular Churches in the universal Church. For Catholic faith, the essential role of the pope is to make visible the universal unity that we profess in the Creed and to make it credible that the different churches with their manifold traditions and even with their tensions are in real and visible communion with each other. This witness of Catholic faith is indispensable for the development of the ecumenical movement.

Finally, there is also disagreement over the role of the Virgin Mary in the mystery of Christ and the Church. All Christians recognize her as the Mother of the Lord, Christ true God and true Man, and they see in her a model for the Church. Still, the Catholic Church also recognizes her role as spiritual Mother of the disciples of Jesus her Son. She intercedes for them and helps them grow in the faith; her maternal mediation participates in the one and only mediation of Christ (John Paul II, *Redemptoris Mater*, no. 38). Mary guides Christians to hear the Word of God.

The quest for the visible unity of Christians is certainly important: unity in the Eucharist, in ministry, and in ecclesial structure. But what the Church needs most of all is to be found holy. Those who seek sanctification through self-denial can play a useful role in working toward reconciliation and unity. Ecumenism today can be authentic and bear the fruits of unity only if it is a movement of sanctification in God's truth and in generosity of heart, an ecumenism of truth in charity.

The Church as Communion

ON THE FIRST ANNIVERSARY OF THE PUBLICATION OF THE LETTER COMMUNIONIS NOTIO

June 15, 1993, marked the first anniversary of the publication of the Letter *Communionis Notio* by the Congregation for the Doctrine of the Faith to the bishops of the Catholic Church on some aspects of the Church understood as communion, approved by John Paul II on May 28, 1992.

Given the brief time that has transpired since its publication, it is still early for a proper evaluation of the document's real impact on the "hoped-for theological investigation," as the *Letter* recalled (no. 2). On the occasion of this first anniversary of its publication, it seems opportune nonetheless to offer a few reflections in light of the first reactions to the *Letter* in Catholic and non-Catholic theological circles as well as among international ecumenical groups.

First of all, it can be noted with satisfaction that the idea of communion has generally been recognized as a suitable notion for understanding the Church in the light of the New Testament sources as the *Letter* set it out in Chapter 1: "The Church, a Mystery of Communion."

In fact, the concept of communion is recognized as especially apt for "expressing the core of the Mystery of the Church, and can certainly be a key for the renewal of Catholic ecclesiology" (no. 1). Many particular aspects addressed in the *Letter* were received and commented upon in a very positive manner: from the Trinitarian roots of *communio* to the ecclesial nature of institutions established by the Apostolic Authority for particular pastoral works, etc. Three central and closely interconnected themes of the *Letter* have, however, been the object of closer and, at times critical, commentary. These now deserve further reflection, given their importance for ecclesiology and ecumenism.

The Universal Church and Particular Churches

Chapter 2 of the *Letter* ("Universal Church and Particular Churches") addresses the theme of expressing the mystery of the Church understood as communion; more specifically, the organic nature of the Church as a communion of Churches (no. 8). In this context, the Letter *Communionis Notio* formulates what could be seen as its interpretive key: the mutual interiority between the universal Church and particular Churches, which is described in the following words: "In order to grasp the true meaning of the analogical application of the term *communion* to the particular Churches taken as a whole, one must bear in mind above all that the particular Churches, insofar as they are 'part of the one Church of Christ,' have a special relationship of 'mutual interiority' with the whole, that is, with the universal Church, because in every particular Church 'the one, holy, catholic and apostolic Church of Christ is truly present and active'" (no. 9).

According to this guiding principle, which some commentators declared a propitious phrase, the particular Churches and the universal Church are both equally considered in the light of a relationship that "cannot be compared to that which exists between the whole and the parts in a purely human group or society" (no. 9). Every particular Church is truly *Church* although not the *whole* Church. At the same time, the universal Church is not distinct from the particular Churches but neither is she the mere sum of them. The "essential mystery" (no. 9) of this relationship is captured in the celebrated conciliar expression *ex quibus et in quibus* (*Lumen Gentium*, no. 23), which the *Letter* develops further with the expression *Ecclesia in et ex Ecclesiis; Ecclesiae in et ex Ecclesia* (no. 9).

This mutual interiority, by means of which in every particular Church the universal Church *exsistit, inest et operatur* (cf. *Lumen Gentium*, no. 23), is what makes the premise built into the entire argument of the *Letter* comprehensible: namely, that the particular Church is a subject complete in itself only when the one, holy, catholic, and apostolic Church is present and active in it; in other words, to the degree to which it possesses interiorly all the links of universal communion. We will return to the consequences of this statement below. First we should clarify one of the points that has evoked some criticism regarding this principle of reciprocal interiority.

There are some who think that *mutual interiority* should be set off in parentheses from the *Letter's* statement that the universal Church "is not the result of the communion of the Churches, but, in its essential mystery, it is a reality *ontologically and temporally* prior to every *individual* particular Church" (no. 9). The question being raised is clear. If, while the Church journeys through history, there is a mutual interiority between the universal Church and the particular Churches, does this mean that the universal Church first existed on its own and then came particular Churches distinct from it? In what sense, then, is the universal Church at the same time immanent and prior to every *individual* particular Church? (We call the reader's attention to this word—*individual*—which the *Letter* even highlights typographically.)

To understand the sense of this statement, as a number of commentators have also pointed out, one must first take into account the paragraph where the *Letter* maintains that it would be "ecclesiological unilateralism" to consider that *first* there is the particular Church while the universal Church "is the result of a *reciprocal recognition* on the part of the particular Churches" (no. 8). Against all this, number 9 quotes John Paul II: "The universal Church cannot be conceived as the sum of the particular Churches, or as a federation of particular Churches." Therefore the *Letter*'s first purpose is to rule out the idea that some sort of *local* Church first emerged in Jerusalem from which other local Churches were gradually formed, which, by slowly coming together, gave rise to the universal Church. To the contrary, recent exegesis points out the oversimplification this idea, rejected by the Letter *Communionis Notio* (and, coincidentally, also in the working document of the Catholic Church and the Ecumenical Council of Churches, *Eglise: Locale et universelle*, no. 22). One cannot deduce from the obvious fact that the expression "*ontological* priority" does not occur in Scripture that its meaning is extra-biblical. Rather, affirmation of the ontological priority of the universal Church over the particular Churches is based on Pauline ecclesiology especially as found in the Letters to the Ephesians and the Colossians.

That having been said, the statement in number 9 needs to be analyzed on its own. The Church characterized as prior is certainly the "Church-mystery," but also the "one Church" that was made manifest on the day of Pentecost. This Church of Jerusalem, whose appearance was defined "locally," was still not a *local* (or *particular*) Church in the current sense of the term; that is, it was not a *portio Populi Dei* (cf. *Christus Dominus*, no. 11), an *individual* particular Church, as the *Letter* says, but the *Populus Dei*, the *Ecclesia universalis* that speaks every language and, in this sense, the mother of all the particular Churches, which would be born of her as daughters through the Apostles.

Perhaps the reason for the occasional misunderstanding of the *chronological priority* that the *Letter* attributes to the universal Church is that the universal Church is all too frequently considered as an abstract reality opposed to the supposedly concrete reality of the particular Church. On the contrary, in this phrase about priority, the *Letter* is considering the universal Church in the most concrete and, at the same time, in the most mysterious manner. The universal Church spoken of here is the Church of Jerusalem at the Pentecost event. Nothing could be more concrete and localized than the 120 gathered there. But the unrepeatable originality and the mystery of the 120 lies in the fact that the *ecclesial structure* that defines them as Church is *the very structure of the universal*

Church. There are the Twelve with Peter at the head and, in communion with them, the whole Church that grows—the five thousand—and that speaks all languages in a moment of unity and universality that is simultaneously as local as can be without being—inasmuch as it is the Church of Pentecost—an "*individual* particular Church" in the current sense of the term. On Pentecost there is no "mutual interiority" of the universal Church and the particular Church, because these two dimensions have not yet appeared as distinct. There is the Christological *ephapax* (cf. Heb 7:27), the anticipation of the eschatological Church, of the Body of Christ *tout court*.

To say that the Church of Pentecost, like Pentecost itself, belongs in some way to the *ephapax* of Christ, to the unrepeatable uniqueness of the salvific event, is also to say that this Church presided over by Peter and, with him, the other Apostles, sets forth the normative manner for the Church to take shape in the future (the Church presided over by the Successor of Peter and, with him, the successors of the Apostles). For the Church revealed at Pentecost, despite its unrepeatable uniqueness, is simply the Church of Christ that we profess in the Creed along with its four marks and that therefore always remains the matrix of the universal Church—understood as *Communio Ecclesiarum*—and of the particular Churches as they exist in the *tempus Ecclesiae*. During this earthly pilgrimage, the universal Church as a historical concept will become the Church of the diaspora, the Church of the Apostles scattered around the world, and the Church of their successors. From this moment on, the historical concept of a particular Church will acquire the sense of having a single Apostle or successors of the Apostles as ministerial head rather than the whole Apostolic College. The *Letter*'s affirmation of the temporal and chronological priority of the universal Church over every individual particular Church can be understood in this sense. Rather than setting the universal Church and the particular Church in contradistinction to each other, it sheds light on the mutual interiority between the universal Church and the particular Church.

Ecclesial Communion, Eucharist, and Episcopacy

In light of the mutual interiority between the universal Church and the particular Churches, the Letter *Communionis Notio* develops a few considerations that derive from it. The first regards incorporation into the Church through baptism, which is described as a single and unique act with a double dimension, universal and local, for which reason "whoever belongs to one particular Church belongs to all the Churches" (no. 10). In this sense, as various comments on the *Letter* have also pointed out appropriately, incorporation into the universal Church is as immediate as incorporation into a particular Church. Membership in the universal Church and membership in a particular Church constitute a single Christian reality.

The *Letter* moves on to describe the Eucharistic character of the Church. The mutual interiority between the universal Church and the particular Churches is realized and expressed to the greatest degree in the celebration of the Eucharist, for the Church is present in its fullness wherever the Eucharist is celebrated, not just the local Church but the *Catholic* Church of which St. Augustine spoke. This is what defines the catholicity of every local Eucharistic celebration. On this point, therefore, the Letter *Communionis Notio* states that the celebration of the Eucharist makes present the totality of the mystery of the Church inasmuch as it also receives and fully experiences all the principles of ecclesial unity and universality that the celebration of the Eucharist itself requires, including the episcopal principle of apostolic succession. Therefore "unity, or communion, between the particular Churches in the universal Church, is rooted not only in the same faith and in the common Baptism, but above all in the Eucharist and in the Episcopate" (no. 11).

The *Letter* continues by setting the Eucharistic reality of the Church and the episcopal ministry in intimate relationship with each other and, within the latter, the Petrine ministry as an intrinsic element of the college of bishops (cf. *Lumen Gentium*, no. 22). Clearly it does not pretend to place the Petrine principle on the same level as the Eucharistic mystery nor to state that this is the only component of ecclesiality. It simply wishes to highlight that every legitimate celebration of the Eucharist by the People of God requires the defining structure of the Church as an organically structured priestly body; hence the bond of communion between the local Church and its bishop, and his bond with his brothers in the episcopacy and with its Head, as a College that gives this apostolic body continued existence (cf. *Lumen Gentium*, no. 22). For this reason communion with the college of bishops is not an element *external* to the Eucharistic celebration nor, consequently, to the very existence of the particular Churches, but is an internal dimension, an *interior* element.

This last statement, a defining feature of the whole document, translates the interiority of the universal Church in the particular Churches, specifically into the level of hierarchic *communio*. Of course, the *Letter* will apply it to the Petrine ministry (no. 13), but note that when the document refers to this internal dimension of the particular Church, it likewise affirms it with respect to the episcopal college as such. Thus there is no hint of "papal unilaterality" in these statements but rather a deepened understanding of the interiority of the organic dimension of the universal Church in the very existence of the particular Church. In this regard, it is noteworthy that this clarification has not always received due consideration: it is the episcopal college with its head that constitutes the element internal to every particular Church for the simple reason that every Church really *is* the Catholic Church in a particular place. At no time does the *Letter* intend to offer a "new" interpretation of the immediate and universal jurisdiction of the Roman Pontiff. Rather, it offers a suitable outline for understanding the relationship between the episcopal college and the pope, as well as between the universal Church and particular Churches.

Ecclesial Communion and Ecumenism

The principle of mutual interiority makes it possible to understand the ecumenical considerations of the *Letter*, which begin by recalling the teaching of the Second Vatican Council on the communion *already existing* (although not yet fully) with non-Catholic Churches and Christian communities. There already exists a communion that allows recognizing the Eastern Orthodox Churches as particular Churches (no. 17). This aspect, which certain comments do not keep sufficiently in mind, is quite relevant. In fact, a particular Church is one in which mutual interiority with the universal Church exists; that is to say, a Church in which the one, holy, catholic, and apostolic Church is present (no. 7). The profound reason for this presence is the Eucharist. Looking back to Decree *Unitatis Redintegratio*, the *Letter* recalls this important statement: "Through the celebration of the Eucharist of the Lord in each of these Churches, the Church of God is built up and grows in stature" (no. 17). The Eucharist, the *Letter* continues, builds up the Church and makes it grow, "for in every valid celebration of the Eucharist the one, holy, catholic and apostolic Church becomes truly present" (no. 17). The *Catholica* is made present in the Eucharistic celebration of these Churches, just as in the celebrations of Churches in full communion with Rome. The importance of these statements is obvious.

The *Letter* must press on in its effort to pierce the *nexus mysteriorum*. Here it points to the doctrine that communion with the pope and with the college are internal instances of the ecclesiality of a particular Church and to its objective manifestation in the celebration of the Eucharist. What the *Letter* wishes to demonstrate is the conviction of the Catholic Church that every valid celebration of the Eucharist builds up and grows the one and only Church, that is the *Catholica*, indivisible in its unity. The Eucharist, for its part, expresses or recalls the full communion with the whole Church, with the universal Church, represented by the episcopal college and its head, the pope (cf. no. 17). It follows that the absence of full communion in the elements of ecclesial unity entails, to a greater or lesser degree (cf. no. 17), a separation that is defined by a common and traditional expression as a *wound*.

This is undoubtedly a very sensitive area, and, especially here, the *Letter* wishes to strike a balance between the clarity of the Catholic faith and the way to present it respectfully. When it affirms that these are indeed particular Churches but that they are wounded because of the absence of full communion with the head of the episcopal college, it intends to say that this is also a wound for the Catholic Church (cf. no. 17), given that "the divisions among Christians prevent the Church from effecting the fullness of catholicity proper to her in those of her sons who, though joined to her by baptism, are yet separated from full communion with her. Furthermore, the Church herself finds it more difficult to express in actual life her full catholicity in all its aspects" (*Unitatis Redintegratio*, no. 4). It cannot be otherwise if the Church that is built up and grows in these Churches is the one Church of Christ. The separation affects us all, and we all share responsibility for it in a measure known only to God. Therefore, everyone needs to make a renewed effort of conversion to the Lord who calls all to be "one flock, one shepherd" (Jn 10:16).

The theological consequences of separation are varied. While the absence of full communion affects the very ecclesiality of these particular Churches, for the Catholic Church, separation affects the expression of its historical catholicity (cf. no. 17). For this reason, the Catholic Church sees itself moved to act in such a way as to make it possible to "recognize the continuity of the Primacy of Peter in his successors, the Bishops of Rome, and to see the Petrine ministry fulfilled, in the manner intended by the Lord, as a worldwide apostolic service, which is present in all the Churches *from within*" (no. 18), in other words, the full communion objectively required by every valid Eucharistic celebration.

It should come as no surprise, as it did for some commentators, that the *Letter* has various explanations for the consequences of incomplete communion between the Catholic Church and the other Churches and Christian communities. Nor can it be characterized as a "hardening" of the doctrinal position of the Catholic Church. The Second Vatican Council was able to say that the Catholic Church believes that the one Church of Christ "constituted and organized in the world as a society, subsists in the Catholic Church, which is governed by the successor of Peter and by the bishops in union with that successor, although many elements of sanctification and of truth can be found outside of her visible structure. These elements, however, as gifts properly belonging to the Church of Christ, possess an inner dynamism toward catholic unity" (*Lumen Gentium*, no. 8). This equation of the Church of Jesus Christ with the Roman Catholic Church should not be taken to mean that there are not elements of sanctity and truth of the *One, Holy* Church outside of it. What the Catholic Church does maintain is its belief that this unity conferred by Christ on his Church from the very beginning "dwells in the Catholic Church as something she can never lose, and we hope that it will continue to increase until the end of time" (*Unitatis Redintegratio*, no. 4). The Second Vatican Council's statement about the relationship between the Catholic Church and the non-Catholic Churches and Christian communities should also be recalled (cf. *Unitatis Redintegratio*, no. 23).

It is therefore hard to understand how certain comments have interpreted the affirmations of the Letter *Communionis Notio* as a pretext for the desire to go beyond the doctrine established by the Second Vatican Council regarding the unity of the Church and the place occupied by the Roman Pontiff in full ecclesiastical communion. The *Letter* merely offers a reminder that considering the primacy of the Bishop of Rome as a defining feature of the Church according to the will of Christ does not amount to a new teaching: "It was to the apostolic college alone, of which Peter is the head, that we believe our Lord entrusted all the blessings of the New Covenant, in order to establish on earth the one Body of Christ into which all those should be fully incorporated who already belong in any way to God's people" (*Unitatis Redintegratio*, no. 3). The Bishop of Rome is inseparable from his brother bishops, just as Peter was from the other Apostles. Peter also receives individually what was conferred on the Twelve including Peter. Therefore, the Second Vatican Council "again proposes" the teaching on papal primacy "to be firmly believed by all the faithful" (*Lumen Gentium*, no. 18). The Catholic Church hopefully desires that this doctrine should be the object of further theological investigation, aware that this primacy, while "preserving its substance as a divine institution, can find expression in various ways according to the different circumstances of time and place, as history has shown" (*Letter*, no. 18).

In the meantime, the Church desires to continue ecumenical dialogue starting from its own ecclesiological identity. This position is not only legitimate but essential to the spirit and the letter of the Second Vatican Council (cf. *Unitatis Redintegratio*, no. 11). On the other hand, the *Letter* decidedly does not intend to encourage those who would back away from the process of rapprochement among Christians, much less to weaken the real ties of communion that already exist between non-Christian Churches and the Catholic Church and form the basis for true ecclesial fraternity. The Catholic Church perseveres in her irrevocable disposition to continue the dialogue already in progress on various questions and, especially, given its obvious ecumenical importance, regarding the ministry of the Successor of Peter and of the whole episcopal college in service to the communion of the Churches.

* * *